web accessibility

practical advice for the library and information professional

edited by **Jenny Craven**

facet publishing

Published by Facet Publishing, 7 Ridgmount Street, London WC1E 7AE
www.facetpublishing.co.uk

Facet Publishing is wholly owned by CILIP: the Chartered Institute of Library and Information Professionals.

British Library Cataloguing in Publication Data
A catalogue record for this book is available from the British Library.

ISBN 978-1-85604-625-1

First published 2008

Typeset from author's disk in 11/14pt University Old Style and Zurich Expanded by Facet Publishing.
Printed and made in Great Britain by MPG Books Ltd, Bodmin, Cornwall.

Contents

Contributors

Simon Ball
Dr Simon Ball is a Senior Advisor with the JISC TechDis Service, which works to provide advice and guidance on technology and disability to promote an accessible and inclusive experience for students and staff in higher, further and adult education across the UK. His work focuses on a range of issues including e-assessment, the accessibility of learning and e-learning materials and web-based resources, mobile learning, and the use of institutional policy to effect change in technology provision for inclusion.

Peter Brophy
Peter Brophy, Director of CERLIM, is Professor of Information Management at Manchester Metropolitan University and a former university librarian. He has directed numerous research projects, including several concerned with accessibility, and has published widely in the field.

Jenny Craven
Jenny Craven is a qualified librarian and has worked as a Research Associate at the Centre for Research in Library and Information Management (CERLIM) for over ten years. She has worked on research projects mainly concerned with web accessibility and usability, with a particular focus on access to information by blind and visually impaired people. She is a Trustee for ForceUK, a charity that seeks to improve access to information and library materials by blind, visually and print impaired people, and is on the Standing Committee of the IFLA Section of Libraries for the Blind.

E. A. Draffan

E. A. Draffan trained as a speech and language therapist before specializing in the field of assistive technologies. She has since worked with disabled students in further and higher education, set up an Assistive Technology Centre, developed a database of assistive technologies and contributed to the work of TechDis and other institutions and groups. She is a Research Fellow at the University of Southampton.

Richard Eskins

After many dubious years as a musician Richard Eskins found salvation in the web while completing a degree in Library and Information Studies at Manchester Metropolitan University in the early 1990s. Remaining in the department from which he graduated, he moved from a support role into teaching and is now a Senior Lecturer. He has been involved in teaching web design, with a focus on usability and accessibility, for over ten years.

Julie Howell

Julie Howell is a passionate advocate for disabled people's right to enjoy everything the web has to offer. Following 12 years campaigning to raise awareness of web accessibility on behalf of RNIB, she received the New Media Age 'Greatest Contribution to New Media' Award, shortly followed by the Net Imperative 'Special Lifetime Achievement' Award. She founded one of the UK's oldest and best loved social networks for people with multiple sclerosis. Now in its twelfth year, 'Jooly's Joint' has a membership exceeding 40,000 worldwide and has received the Yell UK Web Award (Mirror Readers' Site) and the *New Statesman* New Media Award for Best Online Community. She is Director of Accessibility at Fortune Cookie.

Brian Kelly

Brian Kelly is the UK Web Focus adviser, based at UKOLN, University of Bath. The post, funded by the MLA (Museums, Libraries and Archives Council) and the JISC (Joint Information Systems Committee), has a remit to advise the cultural heritage and higher and further education sectors on standards and best practices related to use of the world wide web. His areas of interest include accessibility and Web 2.0. Since 2004 he has published a series of peer-reviewed papers on accessibility. The initial paper, 'Developing a Holistic Approach for E-Learning Accessibility' by Kelly, Phipps and

Swift, introduced a holistic approach to e-learning accessibility. These ideas have since been further developed. He was awarded a prize for the best research paper at the ALT-C 2005 conference.

David Sloan

David Sloan is Project Lead of the Digital Media Access Group, a research and consultancy unit based in the School of Computing at the University of Dundee. Since 1999 he has specialized in promoting inclusive design of websites and other information and communication technologies by providing services such as accessibility audits and user evaluations on a commercial basis, while also conducting research into effective ways of promoting accessible design techniques. In 2006 he completed a PhD that investigated how web accessibility evaluation methods can best influence website designers to develop a greater empathy with and understanding of accessible design.

Chapter 1

Introduction

JENNY CRAVEN

The rationale for *Web Accessibility: practical advice for the library and information professional* is to provide a practical introduction to web accessibility for library and information professionals, students and lecturers. The subject is an important one because of the increasing provision of resources in an electronic format, in particular via the world wide web, together with raised awareness of the importance of widening access for all. Increasingly, recognition is given to the fact that it is a moral duty as well as a legal requirement to take reasonable steps to ensure that no one is excluded from access to goods and services, including access to web-based information and resources, and that it also makes good business sense to widen the customer base. Although there is an abundance of advice and guidelines available on the subject of web accessibility and usability, this book aims to provide practical advice from a range of experts and practitioners in this area, covering the issues relevant to the library and information sector.

The term 'accessibility' can mean different things to different people. In the library environment it can relate to the library functions and 'ensuring that all services are usable by all users' (Brophy, 2007). Libraries should be physically accessible and sensitive to the needs of users, and there are a number of recommendations for this, including:

- attention to site planning and car parking
- improving entrance doors

- internal planning, such as doors, handrails, staircases and lifts
- attention to colour schemes, lighting and signage
- provision of telephones, adapted toilets, and adapted windows
- attention to floor surfaces and floor coverings
- design of reception areas
- attention to safety procedures.

The technological aspects of the library should also be accessible. This could include accessibility between:

- different technologies: operating system (such as MS Windows), application (such as Excel, Word, or a web browser) and assistive technology (AT) where necessary (such as screen magnification or a screenreader)
- different technologies and humans: achieved using a combination of the above and via a user interface
- humans, technology and the context of the interaction: achieved via a combination of the above, and within the context of the interaction (such as e-resources/materials, virtual learning environments, repositories, borrower transactions etc.). (Adapted from Holbye, 2007)

The library should be 'virtually' accessible, and so the library website should be designed according to accessibility guidelines and should provide information about opening times, services offered and contact details. It should also provide access to the catalogue, online journals, abstracts and contents pages, as well as to borrower details, renewal and reservation services. The provision of full-text journal articles and the development of e-book provision can mean increased opportunities to access library services remotely. This will be further enhanced by the continuing implementation of copyright legislation that allows alternative formats designed for people with visual or other impairments to be produced from digital files without payment of a fee.

Web accessibility generally refers to the application of technical solutions to the design of a website in order to render it more accessible to users. Draffan (Chapter 2) describes the different types of tools that can be used to help widen access to the web. These tools include functions already built into the operating system, such as the ability to change the display settings to high-contrast colours for text and background, with enlarged fonts, or to adapt keyboard, mouse and sound settings. Other tools include those that are often referred to as 'enabling' or 'assistive' technologies provided by third parties. These are separate software applications (often, but not exclusively, provided by commercial companies) that can be loaded onto the computer to support the hardware or add other functionality such as Braille translation for an embosser, screen magnification, or screenreading with high-quality speech synthesis. The issue of individual customization of the desktop and user profiles is also discussed in Chapter 2, looking in particular at the problem of customization within networked environments.

Accessibility between technologies (operating system, application and assistive technology) will help to widen access to the web for many people when used in combination with accessible web design. How accessible web design affects different people is explored by Ball (Chapter 3), beginning with a discussion of the concept of 'Design for All', which encourages the designer to consider the full range of needs (including technological, informational and accessibility) and characteristics the audience will exhibit and to cater for them accordingly. With this in mind, Ball explains the importance of considering the 'purpose' of the website and how it will be accessed (e.g. via a computer, a mobile device, a user with low internet connection speed, or a combination of these). The different needs and characteristics of the likely audience of the website are explored, suggesting different mobility, visual, audio, cognitive and technological needs, and how access can be improved through accessible web design techniques such as layout, navigation and the provision of images and multimedia.

Chapters 2 and 3 having established how to widen access to the web through the use of assistive technologies and display adjustments, and through accessible design techniques that help to address different user needs, Sloan (Chapter 4) considers the importance of accessible web design. This includes social, financial, technical and legal factors, all of which provide a strong case for the adoption of accessible web design techniques and the development of accessibility statements and policies. Despite the strong arguments in favour, a number of barriers to accessibility have also been identified. These include the perceived cost of accessible design, fears about the loss of creative design, a lack of legislative clarity, and a lack of organizational support. The barriers are discussed, together with possible solutions to help eliminate them.

Barriers described in Chapter 4 may also be attributed to a lack of understanding of issues relating to accessible web design, and an overview of the advice and guidance available to help counteract this is provided by Howell (Chapter 5). Beginning with a brief history of accessible web design, this chapter includes an explanation of how the correct application of properly validated coding such as Hypertext Mark-up Language (HTML) or Extensible Hypertext Mark-up Language (XHTML), which define the structure of the content, together with the use of Cascading Style Sheets (CSS), which define the way the content is displayed, can aid the accessibility of the website or web-based resource. Howell outlines some established sources of advice and guidance on accessibility, such as the different guidelines provided by the World Wide Web Consortium (W3C) Web Accessibility Initiative (WAI), together with suggestions for keeping up to date with web accessibility issues and recommendations.

The initial chapters having established how to widen access to the web and why this is important, Sloan (Chapter 6) then considers the different methods available to evaluate and assess the accessibility of websites, which is also an important part of accessible web design, whether as part of a new design project or as an assessment of an existing resource to identify potential barriers. A variety of effective techniques for evaluating a website's accessibility are identified, including automated, manual and user techniques; the pros and cons of each are discussed, with a recommendation for using a hybrid method in order to adopt a more holistic approach to accessibility assessment. Sloan recommends this approach because it offers the best balance in terms of resources required and the range and quality of results. Identifying accessibility problems is only part of the picture, however, and Sloan goes on to suggest how they can be reported in ways that are helpful to those responsible for removing or reducing the barriers identified. He covers methods of conducting an accessibility audit and reporting the results effectively so as to identify what actions are required, why they are required and the level of importance attributed to each action.

Whereas many of the chapters in this book can be of general relevance to anyone interested in accessible web design, Brophy (Chapter 7) brings together a number of issues directly related to library and information services. Specific problems faced by library and information professionals are identified, including limited budgets, conflicting demands, and difficulties in employing staff dedicated solely to accessibility. To help address these and other problems, Brophy recommends adopting a sevenfold strategy which comprises time taken to listen to the user community, becoming familiar with key sources of advice and guidance, developing an accessibility policy, conducting accessibility audits, developing a strategy to action improvements, providing appropriate assistive technologies, and continuously monitoring and reviewing what is being achieved. Other accessibility issues discussed in this chapter are digitization of web-based materials, provision and procurement of third-party content, and the growing use of Web 2.0 technologies in libraries.

The issues and recommendations covered in Chapter 7 can also be linked to Chapter 8, where Eskins and Craven discuss the education and training of library and information professionals in accessible web design and the provision of 'Design for All' in the curriculum. Recommendations that have been made to the software industry, that all web designers must be trained in Design for All (DfA) accessibility requirements and techniques, have been addressed to some extent, and examples are given of the types of web accessibility training and online courses available, with discussion of their relevance to library and information professionals. As well as looking at the provision of relevant training, there is discussion of the need to ensure students of all web design and web authoring related courses receive training in web accessibility as a core part of the module or curriculum, rather than it being provided as an add-on for those already in the job market. Examples of good practice of where this is already taking place in the LIS curricula are given.

Examples of good practice form the basis of Chapter 9, where Craven demonstrates, through evidence of improving access to resources, and the implementation of recommendations provided by the IFLA checklist on access to libraries for persons with disabilities, how web accessibility is being addressed by library and information professionals. Despite the examples of good practice, Craven reveals that there is still a gap in the awareness of issues relating to web accessibility, as demonstrated in surveys and studies, but that there is evidence that this gap is being addressed through a number of initiatives and action plans. Examples are also provided in this chapter of studies undertaken to improve and encourage access for all, including the importance of involving users in the process.

Looking to the future, Kelly (Chapter 10) takes a critical look at some of the developments in web accessibility guidelines and assessment, and provides some suggestions as to how these could be improved, in particular through a more holistic approach to web accessibility. Starting with an overview of the holistic approach developed to address the accessibility of e-learning materials, he broadens this out to consider other areas such as communication, entertainment and the storage and retrieval of information. He also considers the accessibility of newly emerging technologies which are being increasingly adopted by library and information professionals, including those referred to as Web 2.0, such as social networking and sharing technologies. Finally, Kelly explores some of the principles for web accessibility that are currently included in the latest guidelines being produced by the World Wide Web Consortium Web Accessibility Initiative (W3C/WAI).

The importance of taking a practical approach to web accessibility is the theme of this book. Key issues are discussed and a number of examples are given to help address them. The aim is to provide practical advice to inform, and to encourage engagement with, anyone who is involved in the provision of accessible and sustainable web services. A vision for the future is that accessibility becomes a fundamental part of the mainstream processes of teaching, and of commissioning, procuring, designing, developing and editing websites, web-based resources and services so that access is widened to as many people as possible according to their preferred method of access, application, location or device.

References

Brophy, P. (2007) *The Library in the Twenty-first Century*, 2nd edn, London, Facet Publishing.

Holbye, S. (2007) Experiences from Training Universal Design. Presentation at the Technology for Participation (T4P) conference, Kristiansand Norway, 25–27 June 2007, www.t4p.no/t4p.no/conference.

Chapter 2

Tools used for widening access to the web

E. A. DRAFFAN

Introduction

This chapter aims to cover some of the tools that can be used to access web-based digital materials. Sadly, it has to be said that not everything that is digital is either accessible or usable and not every tool is able to solve the problems that may arise for some users. 'Negroponte (1995) points out a universal truth of the computer age, that merely because a piece of printed text can be converted to a digital format that is accessed in the general sense of the term, does not make the same piece of text accessible to someone for whom the "general sense of the term" does not apply' (Berkowitz, 2006). In this case, 'accessible' means available to those with disabilities using the web.

Accepting that digital access can be compromised, it is important to appreciate the skills and abilities required to use the technologies that enable disabled users to make the most of the huge variety of web-based content. Coyne and Nielsen (2001) point out that even technologically able blind surfers using screen readers could take up to six times longer to reach items, and those using magnification software, which enlarges text and graphics, may take three times longer compared with those surfing without assistive technologies. It takes time to learn to 'auditorily' scan pages at 300 plus words per minute or trawl through pages constantly using the vertical and horizontal scroll bars. It helps us all to have bite-sized chunks of information presented in a natural flow on a series of well-ordered pages.

There are some easy-to-use assistive or enabling technologies with simple menus and instant keyboard access, mouse control, screen reading or magnification. However, there are times when these tools fail to fulfil the needs of disabled people accessing complex materials provided within rich multimedia settings. Technologically able users may use programs that have a wide range of keyboard shortcuts with linking macros and 'work-arounds' that require patience and persistence to automate.

On the other hand, there are also users for whom choosing the right combination of assistive technology solutions, offered as part of a computer's operating system, may be all that is needed to ease reading and access to web-based content. These tools are sometimes hidden when working on local network systems or may be locked down on workstations. Customized user accounts can be arranged, but technical support services are sometimes concerned about allowing users to have access to control panels etc.

Recently introduced portable systems such as pen drives using universal serial bus (USB) connections can carry utilities or complete programs that will operate in the same way as the accessibility suites on most computers. These tend to allow for font and colour changing, magnification, text to speech and screen reading. This may be one way round some of the difficulties encountered on networks.

Computer accessibility using operating system adjustments

Operating system adjustments can provide the user features that can enhance accessibility and usability. For example, high contrast colours for text and background with enlarged fonts are features found in Microsoft Windows operating systems[1] along with Apple[2] and Linux.[3] Depending on the age of the system these additions may be hidden within control panels, given different names, and provide different levels of support. So what may have been known as an accessibility wizard in Windows XP or 2000, becomes the 'Ease of Access Center' in Windows Vista.[4] Apple Mac offer 'VoiceOver'[5] and those using open source systems may have the downloadable 'GNOME Accessibility Project',[6] which is a collection of enabling utilities designed by various developers.

There are some similarities between all the systems in that they provide means for changing keyboard and mouse features, screen reading, magnification, colour and desktop settings.

Keyboard settings

Keyboard settings are used to adapt keyboard-to-screen interactions for those with dexterity and mobility impairments. They may also help individuals who have repetitive strain injuries or other issues that make typing difficult. A simple setting found under the general keyboard settings on all the operating systems provides a method for slowing and delaying the repeat rate at which keys are depressed.

StickyKeys is a way of using key combinations with only one finger or stylus. So, for instance, a shortcut for printing may be 'Ctrl (or Apple) + P' but with StickyKeys enabled each key can be pressed separately. The set-up can also be applied to other keys such as Shift and Alt. StickyKeys can be helpful when form filling on the web and when tabbing back up a page of links, when two keys need to be used together, e.g. Shift + Tab.

There are times when using maps online, animations and other visual technologies that have mouse driven controls such as zoom in and zoom out, where key combinations work to enlarge the entire page, but do not work on a particular area of, for example a map or graphic.

FilterKeys ignores repetitive actions that may be caused by a tremor or unsteady hand. So, if a key is depressed several times the system will not respond to the action after one press. FilterKeys can also provide audible alerts when keys are pressed. Additionally, pressure settings can be adjusted to suit the user by selecting the number and speed of depressions before the action is automatically stopped by the computer.

ToggleKeys provide an auditory alert when a key such as Caps Lock or Num Lock has been pressed. Again, the settings can be altered to suit the user. This utility may also be helpful for those with visual impairments.

SerialKeys provide a way for those who require other input devices, such as single-press switches, joysticks and flat, keyless-concept keyboards, to link to the system. This access is necessary when a communication port is used rather than a universal serial bus (USB) system and, in many cases, has become unnecessary on most systems. The 'SerialKeys software is also designed to allow an augmentative and alternative communication device to communicate with the computer through a serial port connection, and changes that information into keyboard or mouse events, just as if the user were typing on the keyboard or using the mouse'.[7]

Onscreen keyboards are driven by software and appear as a separate screen overlay. The overlay provides access to keys through use of a mouse or by single-key or switch access to the characters and navigational elements. The versions provided by Windows, and by GOK[8,9] within Linux, do not have word prediction, so cannot increase typing speeds for those with mobility or dexterity impairments, but they do provide basic accessibility. For Mac users the onscreen keyboard is an add-on, as it is not provided as part of the operating system.

The problem with onscreen keyboards is that they take up virtual desktop space, so the user may need a larger monitor to be able to read comfortably and navigate around web pages and to reduce excessive scrolling.

Cursor blink rates

Another setting, found under the general keyboard settings on all the operating systems, provides a method for changing the blink rate of the cursor. Being able to nullify the blinking or flashing of objects on web pages is helpful for some people with visual sensitivity problems and certain types of epilepsy. Guideline 7 of World Wide Web Consortium (W3C) Web Content Accessibility Guidelines (WCAG) version 1.0[10] or Guideline 2.3 in version 2.0[11] advises developers to allow users to avoid content that could cause seizures due to photosensitivity, and this includes blink rates, refresh rates on pages as well as items that flicker or flash across the screen. It is possible to see if a web page has these issues by using a flickering check tool.[12] (See Chapter 5 for further details about W3C and WCAG).

Mouse settings

Mouse settings depend on the hardware used as well as the system accessibility options, but are useful for those with dexterity problems, and also when choosing to use the mouse left or right handed, where there are two buttons available.

Mouse button settings provide the option to swap the action button (which is usually double clicked) from the left side to the right to suit a left-handed user. It is also possible to slow or speed up the device's reaction to mouse clicks, which may help those who find the double-click action difficult. When surfing the web single clicks are usually sufficient for most actions.

There are many alternative mouse pointer schemes available, either included within an operating system or as part of an add-on package.

These may provide the user a choice of styles, along with the option to enlarge the pointer or cursor, slow its blink rate and change its colour. All these features can help when locating the pointer while interacting with the computer.

MouseKeys allows for the use of the numeric pad to navigate on the computer rather than the mouse. With a control key such as Num Lock to toggle the feature on and off, by using the middle numbers on a key pad (or those numbers that are linked to functions on the main keyboard of a laptop) the user has control for up, down and diagonal pointer movement.

ClickLock is available with some hardware and software and can be very useful for those with dexterity problems because the mouse button need not be held down while dragging an object from one place to another across the screen. The button can just be clicked, the object moved, and the button clicked again to release the action. This feature can be very helpful if the system provides no alternative to drag and drop type operations.

Scroll wheel is a feature of some mouse devices, incorporating a rotary dial to scroll vertically or horizontally around the screen, or perhaps zoom in and out of a magnified region of the screen. It is often possible to adjust the sensitivity of the scroll wheel to suit the user's comfort and dexterity.

Sound settings

Not all users can hear system alerts and other program warnings. Incorporated into the Windows system are alternatives such as SoundSentry. The Mac has VisualAlert, where application borders pulse as an alert is sounded. Also, on Windows ShowSounds a caption is displayed when a specific warning or voice command is used. These types of support aid those with hearing impairments but also alert users when sound systems are turned off. Visual or sound warnings can be set up when changes occur to the system such as receipt of new messages, or beeps to indicate system errors, or sounds to indicate change in status. Sounds can also be channelled through a cable connection to loop systems and other radio listening devices.

These alerts and text alternatives cannot be adapted for use with web pages that may have video content or with podcasts with audio files. The latter need to provide easy access to volume controls. Closed captions with real-time text generation and audio descriptions are still required. Free programs such as those offered by National Center for Accessible Media

(NCAM) Magpie[13] and CC for Flash[14] are available for developers, and Mac's QuickTime video player can also take display captions.[15]

Display settings

These settings allow for changes to be made to the entire visual appearance of the desktop and many applications. Some users have their own preferences as to how they wish to view programs and may make general text size and font type alterations.

High contrast mode (where text and menu features can be seen in white or yellow on a black background) is available through the accessibility options on most machines as well as via the desktop settings. These settings may provide background and window colour changes as well as screen resolution options. Cathode ray tube (CRT) monitors allow the user to enlarge everything that is viewed by reducing the resolution to, say, 640 × 480 pixels. There are options to change resolution on flat screens, such as those using thin-film transistor (TFT) technology, but the range of optimal resolutions available on a TFT monitor tends to be smaller compared with those found on CRT monitors.

Touch-screen monitors are often used to access catalogues and information about a location or course. The content has to be adapted to suit those with tremors or poor motor control. Speech output can help, but these systems are often not accessible to those with visual impairments.

Certain types of visual impairments may mean a computer user needs to peer very closely at the screen. Frequent breaks will be needed to prevent eyestrain, but it also helps to have content that is divided up between several pages rather than one long column of text and graphics.

Text changes are available in individual applications, including browsers, for viewing web pages with, for example, enlarged fonts, and changed background text and colours. However, for some web pages, such as those designed in certain ways using Adobe Macromedia Flash, Java and other proprietary tools, users will be unable to adjust the look and feel of the content.

Where web pages have been designed with accessibility in mind, more radical changes can be made. Each browser does this in a different way. The BBC's 'My Web My Way'[16] pages offer guidance on how to make surfing easier using a Windows, Mac or Linux system. The latest browsers also allow for general magnification instead of individual text changes, so the entire page, including the graphics, can be magnified to a very high degree.

Magnification

Magnification is offered in many browsers with the enlargement of graphics and text within web pages. However, this option may not offer easy reading for those with more complex visual impairments and who may need particular types of viewing pattern, e.g. masked areas of a page to avoid distraction. The Microsoft Windows operating system provides a magnification bar across the screen, an enhanced area around the mouse, or sections of a viewing area but not the complete desktop. The Apple Mac OS X Leopard system has a zoom feature within VoiceOver that offers complete magnification, high contrast options, and cursor and pointer adaptations. Linux systems have access to free open source programs such as Gnopernicus[17] as part of the Gnome Accessibility Project. Once again, the entire desktop and chosen applications are magnified.

Total screen magnifiers when used with text and graphics at more that four times the usual size involve much more scrolling and searching for items. It is very easy to become disorientated, so it is important to include objects or links that provide context, with plenty of white space. The use of symbols that are repeated throughout a site can be helpful, not just to those with visual impairments but also for dyslexic users or those for whom English is a second language.

Colour can be very important when using magnification, as it can act as a marker to sections of a website as well as to links, but it is equally important to remember that those who are colour-blind need to have different shapes as well as colour. Third-party, more complex, magnification software programs have filters and options for changing colours that can help many users, especially those with specific preferences for reading text on different backgrounds.

Screen reading

Blind computer users invariably have their chosen screen reading software set up to work with all aspects of the system, including navigation, text reading and voice output for actions such as typing or accessing other parts of the operating system. The Microsoft Windows Narrator speech output provides support during installation and when using a basic text editor and navigation controls, but it does not work with all applications on the computer. VoiceOver for the Apple Mac, or Orca[18] for the Linux system, work with most applications but do not have as many user options as the commercial screen readers available for the Windows system.

There is no way for a blind person to follow the context of items on a page without working down the entire contents. It is often the 'search box' that is the first stopping off point. This needs to be at the top of the page, involve minimal scrolling, and be well labelled. If there are graphics without explanations and important information is not given at the beginning it can take a long time for the person to understand what is required. Neal Ewers of the Trace Research and Development Center comments:

> Just the other day I was reading something that made no sense to me whatsoever until I got to about what I assume the middle of the page was, and then what was on the middle of the page said 'Read the text below and use these instructions to fill out the top part of the page'. Well geeze, you know if I had seen, I would have gone right there. But my problem as a screen reader user is I can't.[19]

To aid the listener, care needs to be taken with abbreviated forms. Acronyms need to be given their original meaning at least once, as screen readers often try to make words out of a collection of letters, so USB may be said as single letters but CAP may sound like a piece of apparel rather than C.A.P. - the Communications Aid Project or a Community Arts Programme. It also helps to have accurate punctuation although this may not always fit in with the requirements of publishers. For example, a full stop at the end of bullet points helps to pause a screen reader. Techno-Vision, specialists in screen reader and Braille technologies, have provided an easy-to-follow guide on the subject.[20]

Reading downloadable Adobe PDF files, which maintain the writer's desired formatting, can also cause problems. There can be problems if the structure of the content is poorly organized. The screen reader may track across columns rather than down them, unless they have been properly tagged with a reading order. Graphics, diagrams or equations without alt tags (alternative text describing the picture) or text descriptions do not help and, once again, these may interfere with the logical flow of the screen reading. Properly tagged PDFs can benefit everyone, providing structure to documents and allowing text to reflow, whatever the size of the monitor.

Speech recognition

Microsoft Windows Vista and Mac OS X both provide integrated speech recognition. The Mac system is more of a voice command application for navigation but Microsoft Vista allows for full dictation in many applications. This may be helpful for user with mobility and dexterity impairments as well as specific learning difficulties such as dyslexia. Forms can be filled in and text-edit boxes completed within the Mozilla Firefox or Internet Explorer browser. The wikis or blogs that have become part of the social networking phenomenon can also be written.

Summary of operating system adjustments

To complete the discussion of individual elements of the operating system adjustments, the following points summarize the key issues that should be taken into account when considering their use to enhance accessibility and usability:

1. All operating systems can facilitate some changes to the way text appears on the screen, with a certain amount of magnification, colour options and, in some cases, speech output.
2. The option to alter the appearance of most applications, with bigger icons and high contrast modes of viewing, is also available.
3. There are work-arounds for those who cannot type on a standard keyboard, options to adjust mouse pointers and cursors, and some visual alerts to sounds that are used for warnings.
4. However, these system utilities rarely provide sufficient assistance for those who are blind or have more complex disabilities.
5. This is when third-party solutions are required but they are not necessarily more complex than those provided by the operating system.

Third-party solutions

Third-party solutions relate to those technologies that are specifically designed for tasks supporting a variety of access needs, from making the keyboard easier to use, to reading text on a screen. These items may be special peripherals or pieces of hardware added to the computer - unlike the support mechanisms provided as part of the operating systems, which tend to be software driven. Software includes applications that are loaded onto the computer and that either support the hardware or provide additional functionality such as Braille translation for an embosser or screenreading with high quality speech synthesis.

Keyboards

There are numerous kinds of keyboards, ranging from those ergonomically designed to persuade users to improve their keyboarding positions, to one-handed chord keyboards that enable speedier input or mini keyboards to help those with limited movement. Concept or programmable keyboards can be adapted to suit user preferences with, for example, quick access to favourite web pages or applications.

For those who are blind or have very poor motor control the keyboard may be the only method of access and it is essential that all navigational elements and menus on web pages are 'keyboard accessible'. The tabbing order must be logical because this helps the user to build up a mental model of the page layout. 'The tab order is the order in which the Tab key moves the keyboard focus from one control or item to the next within a dialog box. For Western languages, the tab order is normally from left to right and top to bottom.'[21]

On some web pages Access Keys are used to allow users to combine keys such as Alt or Ctrl plus a letter, so as to jump to a specific target, such as the beginning of a form. The problem is that these keyboard combinations differ between operating systems, browsers and websites, and may conflict with access technologies such as the screenreaders JAWS or SuperNova, which use literally hundreds of these combinations.

Keyboard guards can prevent inaccurate key strokes and can be used by someone with a tremor or poor co-ordination.

Reducing the number of actions needed to access features on a web page can be very helpful, for example avoiding Flash introduction pages or pop-up advertisements. These can cause considerable frustration for slow keyboard users and for screenreader users who may not realize why they are unable to move to the main page.

Scanning software is sometimes needed when a person with severe mobility difficulties uses a single button or switch as a method of inputting data. (This is not to be confused with the optical character recognition software used to access text from books with a hardware scanner often linked to screen-reading software.) This scanning software looks a bit like an onscreen keyboard. For entering text a grid across the screen allows the user to work their way, in a stepped manner with each click on the switch, both vertically and horizontally to the target areas. The switch can also be used in the same way to access points on a web page. Once again, this is made easier if the layout and navigational elements are clear.

Mouse devices, trackballs, joysticks and other pointers

There is a huge variety of mouse-related input devices, from the ergonomically designed versions to large trackballs that may suit users with stiff hands or poor mobility. Some can be set up in different ways, for example using drag lock so the user doesn't have to hold down a button. Gamers may use joysticks, but they also provide better directional control for some users with poor co-ordination and awkward movements. Head pointers, often interacting with a camera, can make navigation difficult but may be the only option for individuals with no or poor limb control. In this case, the head control has to be relatively stable and it is important to check for neck and shoulder pain.

It is beneficial for most mouse users to have well spaced navigational elements - plenty of white space around items so that miss-hits don't send surfers out to other areas and further slow their progress. The size of the target/button, which should be easy to see and hit, is also important.

Screenreader and text-to-speech applications

The Windows operating system has the most third-party software packages available to users for reading from a screen with audio output. Commercial screenreaders such as JAWS,[22] Window-Eyes, SuperNova[23] and Thunder[24] (available free to blind users) provide the user a choice of how to have items read via a speech synthesizer on the computer. The type of voice, speed, pitch, language and amount of punctuation or navigation verbalized can all be altered to suit the user. Many different keyboard shortcuts will tell the user where they are on a page, what they are reading, and more about the context as well as the content. It is possible to have links listed and to skip navigational elements.

The free web browsers Opera[25] and WebbIE[26] provide an indication as to how content can be presented to a screenreader user. This in no way replaces the actual use of screenreading applications when testing pages for accessibility or working with disabled users to identify barriers to access, but they are a rough guide. The browsers will render pages in text-only format so that they flow in a linear progression. There is no chance of a visual scan over the entire page, but rather an auditory skip through links, headings and paragraphs or page elements. This means these features become vital indicators for the user and, in the case of links, must be well described when out of context or be possible to 'skip' altogether if they are repetitive. Headings must be well organized so that there is a natural flow of content, with important items appearing at the top of pages.

Text-to-speech users working with digital materials tend to have reasonably good sight but may have specific learning difficulties, such as dyslexia, which can make reading large amounts of text an issue. There may be visual perceptual difficulties involving, for example, tracking words and phrases. The facility to listen to items while following the content but not be distracted by having all the navigational elements read (as with a screenreader) can be very helpful. Some programs, such as Texthelp Read and Write[27] and ClaroRead,[28] also provide text highlighting and increased letter and line spacing. Once again, it is the combination of the amount of accessibility offered on the web pages and the skills of the user that makes these tools effective. The tools tend to be easier to use with a mouse - for instance choosing the text that is to be read aloud - although some have keyboard shortcuts.

Some websites provide links to programs that will read and highlight the text in various colours, for example Browsealoud[29] and ReadSpeaker,[30] but these tools only operate on web pages and are not complete desktop solutions.

There are other downloads that can be added as toolbars within browsers as well as to applications such as Word. Some are free, for example NaturalReader,[31] or specific to a browser, such as CLiCK, Speak for Mozilla Firefox. These applications tend to use the clipboard in the same way that Safari on the Apple Mac has simple speech output, but usually the text needs to be highlighted before it can be spoken.

In recent years personal digital assistants or electronic organizers and smart mobile phones have begun to offer access to the web with screen-reading or text-to-speech software such as Pocket Hal.[33] The screens are small, but it is also possible to use magnification software such as that provided by the Code Factory[34] and Nuance Zooms.[35]

Braille output

Refreshable Braille displays sit underneath the keyboard with a series of Braille cells made up of moving pins and control buttons. Eighty Braille cells, which look a little like a line of very small dominos, provide the user with one line of information from most computer screens. The lines of text wrap on a smaller Braille display, just as they do on a small screen. They require considerable tactile skills but act in a similar way to screen readers when a blind person is surfing the web. They are often used alongside speech output so well laid-out, text versions of web pages are needed. Thinking of the way a web page may be printed out line by line without graphics may help. If tables and other data layouts can have row and column headings this helps the Braille and screen reader user to work logically through the content.

Speech recognition

Dragon NaturallySpeaking Professional[36] offers a considerable number of additional features when compared with operating system speech recognition programs. It has a mouse grid control system for total hands-free operation. iListen[37] for Mac works in all Apple applications, not just those that are part of the Mac OS. Free voice-command software is also available for Linux, but IBM ViaVoice, which offered full dictation for Linux, is no longer supported.

Summary of third-party solutions

Despite the fact that many third-party solutions enable increased access to computers, the following points highlight some key issues that should be taken into account when considering them to enhance accessibility and usability:

- Developers of web pages and assistive technologies need to be aware that, to work effectively, it is important that users can access information both quickly and efficiently.
- For some, navigational and content barriers have increased as the web has become a more collaborative affair with individual innovation and multiple formats. Assistive technologies need to keep pace with the changes and be easy to learn, so that individuals can concentrate on tasks rather than on technicalities.

Network solutions: individual customization and user profiles

As with all technologies, the users want to be in control! This may be a problem when individuals need to combine assistive technologies with other software and the applications are installed on a network. Some assistive technologies require access to specific user files, for instance voice folders for speech-recognition programs. It is important to set up accessible folders that can be updated and backed up and, if possible, for the user not to be always dependent on a technician's help.

There may be problems with the number of licences or Access Keys available, and how many users can use the technologies at once. Clear instructions to users can alleviate concerns and, with the advent of USB pen-drive versions of software, there may be other options available.

There may be differences of opinion about security requirements versus the ability to change settings and how to manage differing levels of access on networked or open access computers. It is not always easy for users to admit that they are having problems viewing or accessing their programs. For such users it would be perhaps easier for a specialist to set up a profile with all the settings in place and which could be adapted as situations changed. However, this is not always possible and there may even be interoperability issues. In some cases specialized software may not work particularly well with elements of another piece of software, such as magnification with speech and scanning.

Nevertheless, many of these problems can be solved, and it is important to be aware that it is often not due to the assistive technologies that a user is unable to join the network, but rather the registration process. If online registration is part of the system, entry fields, combo-boxes and radio buttons (to name but a few of the elements often found in a registration document) need to be labelled correctly. It is also much easier for most assistive technology users to have an e-mail activation system rather than a 'CAPTCHA' that requires the user to type the letters of a distorted image into a text box.

Once registered and part of the networked community, some websites offer user preferences and these are sometimes saved as cookies or stored in a database, but not all computer services allow cookies to remain on the system. User preferences may also be site specific and so have to be set up on all the most used sites. These adjustments may be all that users require to enable them to access the web and can be achieved with relative ease.

Conclusion

Axel Schmetzke, in a *Library HiTech* article, reiterates some key facts relating to assistive technologies:

- Assistive technologies alone cannot overcome the barriers that are created at a more basic level: the format in which content is presented.
- If not properly formatted or designed, web pages are not accessible to people with certain disabilities - no matter how much assistive technology they may have (Schmetzke, 2001).

It may also be true to say that it is not always the most complex technologies that provide a solution. If the web page layout and formatting can both be kept accessible, clean, clearly understandable and clutter free, then often the most simple-to-use solutions can be adopted. However, assistive technologies have to remain in step with the latest computer-based innovations to provide flexible and efficient access for their users. In the hands of technologically able individuals, these hardware and software systems have proved over the years to be life changing.

The barriers encountered by disabled users are usually due to their working environment rather than their inability to work around the issues. In nearly every case, changes that are made to suit these users have benefits for us all. For example, in 2006 the accessible Tesco shopping site made up 5% of the store's online grocery business:

> I am a continuous user of my PC and consider myself PC literate, and I also consider myself a power-user and am very happy when I am not forced to use the mouse. I actually prefer the accessible site for doing basic shopping as it is fast, clear and easy to use and I can keep my fingers on the keyboard.[38]

Tim Berners-Lee, in a presentation to the United States House of Representatives in March 2007, said:

> So how do we plan for a better future, better for society? We ensure that both technological protocols and social conventions respect basic values. That the Web remains a universal platform: independent of any specific hardware device, software platform, language, culture, or disability.[39]

References

Berkowitz, D. J. (2006) *Stabilizing the Concepts of Digital and Access*, unpublished.

Coyne, K. and Nielsen, J. (2001) *Beyond ALT Text: making the web easy to use for users with disabilities*, Freemont, CA, Nielsen Norman Group, www.nngroup.com/reports/accessibility (accessed 10 April 2007).

Negroponte, N. (1995) *Being Digital*, New York, Alfred A. Knopf.

Schmetzke, A. (2001) Web Accessibility at University Libraries and Library Schools, *Library Hi Tech*, **19** (1), 35–49.

URLs

1 www.microsoft.com/enable
2 www.apple.com/accessibility
3 http://larswiki.atrc.utoronto.ca/wiki
4 www.microsoft.com/enable/products/windowsvista
5 www.apple.com/macosx/features/voiceover
6 http://developer.gnome.org/projects/gap
7 http://trace.wisc.edu/docs/mac_sk_quicksheet/sk_quick.htm
8 www.microsoft.com/enable/training/windowsxp/soundsentry.aspx
9 www.gok.ca
10 www.w3.org/TR/WAI-WEBCONTENT
11 www.w3.org/TR/WCAG20
12 www.webaccessibile.org/test/check.aspx
13 http://ncam.wgbh.org/webaccess/magpie
14 http://ncam.wgbh.org/webaccess/ccforflash
15 www.webaim.org/techniques/captions/quicktime
16 www.bbc.co.uk/accessibility
17 www.gnome.org/learn/access-guide/2.14/sysadmin-6.html
18 http://live.gnome.org/Orca/FrequentlyAskedQuestions
19 www.doit.wisc.edu/accessibility/video/intro.asp
20 www.techno-vision.co.uk/10_Word_Guidelines.htm
21 www-03.ibm.com/able/guidelines/software/swkbdequiv.html
22 www.freedomscientific.com/fs_products/software_jaws.asp
23 www.yourdolphin.com/products.asp
24 www.screenreader.net
25 www.opera.com
26 www.webbie.org.uk
27 www.texthelp.com

28 www.clarosoftware.com
29 www.browsealoud.com
30 www.readspeaker.com
31 www.naturalreaders.com/download.htm
32 http://clickspeak.clcworld.net
33 www.adapt-it.org.uk/products/pockethalpdascreenreader.asp
34 http://codefactory.es/en
35 www.nuance.com/zooms
36 www.nuance.com/naturallyspeaking/professional
37 www.macspeech.com
38 www.it-analysis.com/business/compliance/content.php?cid=8303
39 http://dig.csail.mit.edu/2007/03/01-ushouse-future-of-the-web.html

Chapter 3

Design for All – how web accessibility affects different people

SIMON BALL

Introduction

The web, possibly more than any development since the discovery of electricity, has the potential to provide and liberate, but there exists also a responsibility for authors and designers to ensure it does not prevent and restrict.

There are a vast variety of types of website with many purposes and myriad audiences. All of these factors play a part in the actions that must be taken to ensure the site is as accessible as is relevant or achievable. A site may be simple or complex, textual or graphical. It may be for marketing or sharing, for information provision or information gathering. It may be for the general public or a subset of them, it may be for a known group of people with known characteristics. These factors must be determined before any consideration of accessibility can be made.

The increasing pervasiveness of ICT into the realm of the library and information professional offers an opportunity for increased engagement with a wider variety of users. In some instances the characteristics of these users are known and can be directly catered for, but in most cases the user audience is not known. The range of potential characteristics and needs across this largely unknown audience is therefore as great as within the general populace, and online resources must be designed and created with this factor very much in mind. This chapter will highlight the effects that good and poor practice can have on the user's experience.

What is 'Design for All'?

In brief, 'Design for All' is the creation of a resource that is accessible to, and usable by, every member of the community for whose use it is intended. However, this very concept is a contentious one. Some would argue that 'Design for All' (along with its equivalent in common usage in North America 'Universal Design') simply means the creation of a single resource that can be accessed and effectively used by every person on the planet. Some would argue that the creation of a range of different resources, all of which are suitable for some users, and which reach all users when taken as a whole, also fits within the definition of 'Design for All'. Then there are those who would argue that 'Design for All' is an inappropriate term, detracting from the real aim, which is to create a web resource that is fit for purpose, and therefore which serves the users for whom it is intended. Other terms have been suggested that more accurately fit the intention, such as 'User-Centred Design' or better still 'User-Sensitive Design' (Newell and Gregor, 2001). To some extent this debate is a side issue. What is important is that when designing or creating a web resource, the designer takes consideration of the full range of needs (including technological, informational and accessibility) and characteristics the audience will exhibit and caters for them accordingly.

It is important to note that the designers and creators of web pages are not expected to be experts in assistive technology - the scope and function of the technologies available are always changing and there are experts who can advise on the way they interact with the web. Rather, web designers should be aware of the ways in which users interact with the web, regardless of the technology they use to do so, and ensure their web pages meet all types of need. If that is done, then the only barrier to a user's access will be technological, and usually in time technological barriers can be overcome with expert assistance.

Establishing purpose

When designing or creating an online resource the first task must be to determine the purpose of the site. This will outline only what the website aims to achieve and what it will deliver to users. There may need to be separate considerations made for short- and long-term usage (for example an initial aim may be to raise awareness of a product or service, and longer term to facilitate easy usage of that product or service). Referring back to the original purpose will also keep any subsequent reviews and modifications relevant and on track.

There are many types of website with an array of different purposes. Olejniczak (2004) categorizes these into: entertainment, communication, information and education. The wishes of those who view a site as being a marketing tool will often initially conflict with those who view it as an information resource, and again with those who see it as an agent of empowerment. These discussions should take place prior to any design commencing, such that the designer has a definitive list of purposes which the site must achieve. Often a delicate balance between several purposes needs to be achieved.

Establishing access

Prior to the design stage a decision also needs to be made as to how and where the site will be accessed. Will it be open access, behind a firewall or password protected, or require user registration or verification? How will the site be accessed - via a computer, a mobile device or a user with low internet connection speed (or all of the above)? This is also a key question when planning the extent of the 'Design for All' commitment.

One document that will prove very helpful towards achieving accessibility for anyone designing or commissioning the design of a website is *Publicly Available Specification 78: Guide to good practice in commissioning accessible websites* (DRC, 2006).

The types of users

Once you have determined the purpose of the site and the physical access to the site in terms of security and devices, you can begin to assess the likely characteristics of the users and plan the design of the site accordingly. If the audience for the website is discrete and known, certain assumptions can be made regarding the likely user characteristics in terms of level of academic ability, for example (such as if the resource will be accessed only by final year undergraduates), or the mode of access (such as if the resource will only be accessible during supervised sessions in particular computer suites). However, assumptions about the user's needs or impairments cannot be made, because not all such needs are evident to the observer. If the audience is much wider or public, then no assumptions can be made at all.

User needs

The user needs that may be expressed by users of a resource are many and varied. Many users may not be aware of some of their needs or characteristics, and many more may have several needs, some of which require apparently conflicting accommodations. However, most can be generalized into the following groups.

Mobility and dexterity needs

Users with mobility and dexterity needs include people who cannot physically access a computer using the conventional input devices (i.e. a keyboard or mouse). It may be considered reasonable to assume that all users will be able to input to a computer using some device, but not to predict what that device may be (for example via voice recognition software, virtual or physical head pointing or screen reading and navigating devices). In its simplest form this means that websites should be navigable and usable by using only the keyboard ('tabbing' from item to item) and by using only a click-input device (for example any data entry boxes should be operable via an onscreen keyboard).

Visual needs

Some users of the resource will have no vision, some will have low vision, some will be able to see only part of the screen at one time (for example if requiring magnification), some will be unable to distinguish certain, or indeed any, colours. These are all issues to consider when putting together a web resource, and usually easy to simulate to some degree to check whether resources are accessible or not.

Auditory needs

Some users of the resource will be deaf and others hard of hearing. This has implications not just for the use of sound in the website (audio and video files and related subtitling or transcription issues, for example), but also in that many deaf users' first language will be British Sign Language (BSL). BSL has a different structure and syntax to written or spoken English (and is recognized as a language in its own right) and so the use of Plain English (for further information on the Plain English Campaign visit the website)[1] will be beneficial to this group, as well as to other users for whom English is not their first language.

Cognitive needs

These can include learning difficulties, learning disabilities and dyslexia. A high proportion of the population has some kind of cognitive need, including a variety of conditions known collectively as dyslexia. Other needs manifest in a variety of ways, such as difficulties with numbers, time or information management, navigation and short-term memory. Clarity of purpose, layout and structure in the web-based resource will aid these users.

Technological needs

Some users will be accessing the web via a mobile device with a small screen - you should test your resource to see how it displays on these devices. Some users may be accessing the web via a slow internet connection - you will need to ensure that any graphics or bandwidth-heavy features are used appropriately and that there is alternative information for those who cannot or do not wish to wait for the material to download. Some users may not have the technical ability or confidence to access or download complex or multimedia content - all content should be appropriately signposted and explained, with complex content available in alternative formats.

Other needs

There are myriad other needs that the user group will feature to some extent. These include needs related to specific conditions such as epilepsy or autism. For example, it is common for people with autism to find flashing displays or repetitive sounds especially distracting, or to experience difficulty in interpreting two-dimensional representations of three-dimensional objects (see the Techdis website[2] for a simulation of this effect).

One important point to note is that all of the good practice techniques described in this chapter to benefit these various groups of users will in fact benefit a much larger proportion of users than simply the groups listed here. Good website design is good for all users (which is why websites should be frequently tested by all constituent stakeholders, both disabled and non-disabled), and that is why this chapter focuses not on disability but on good (inclusive) practice.

The effects of good and bad practice

Layout

Keeping layout simple will benefit a range of users:

- Keeping to the same structure on every page will enable users who have difficulties with the language or with reading the text on menu items to become familiar with the appearance or location of the items they require.
- Providing sufficient 'white space' (not necessarily white, but blank) will train the eye of the user towards where they need to go - this is of particular use for some people with dyslexia who have difficulty scanning a page for the items of interest. (Note that the use of white space does not mean the site has to be boring!)
- Blind and visually impaired users will be able to become familiar with a straightforward layout and will be able to navigate more quickly through the site.
- Those with cognitive needs will be able to follow the structure more easily (as will everybody else).

Navigation

Everyone will benefit from a clear, consistent and obvious layout. There should not be too many different menus and menu items on the home page - a short menu of 'housekeeping' items such as 'about us' and 'contact details' and a navigation menu of up to 12 items for content should be the maximum for inclusive navigability. The 'housekeeping' items should be kept to the end of the navigation process, as many more users are interested in 'content' than 'housekeeping'. The exception to this may be an early and prominent placing of the accessibility information page.

Menus and links

There needs to be a careful balance struck between the number of menu items on each page and the number of clicks required to reach each piece of information. It is often stated that everything should be reachable within three clicks from the home page (for example, Zeldman, 2001) because users will become bored and 'click off' if things are made too difficult for them. It is certainly true that this structure would be easier for those who struggle to input clicks or those who struggle with complex layers of structure. However, for others this has meant the creation of other problems - for example blind, visually impaired and some dyslexic users find it difficult to scan a page that contains a large number of links (Brazier and Jennings, 1999) (although this can be sidestepped to some extent by the inclusion of a 'skip navigation' option). So the most inclusive answer is to have a very clear and obvious site structure and navigation (that is the same irrespective of the page the user is on), aided by a breadcrumb trail where possible, that keeps the number of links on each page to a manageable number, and if users need to make more than three clicks to reach their destination it should be obvious at all times where they are in that structure. The inclusion of a breadcrumb trail (breadcrumb trails show links to previous pages the user has navigated through to arrive at the current page, e.g. Home Page Name > Section 1 Name > Subsection 1.1 Name . . .) will then enable users who have become 'lost' to choose which level to return to in order to find their way, including the home page.

Site maps

In addition, it can be extremely valuable to all users to have a clear site map available on a website. This enables users who can visualize an overview of the site to obtain a quick indication of the relationship between items in the site, and can also be used as a navigation aid. Bear in mind that some users will not be able to comprehend the site map and that it may be too complex for screenreader users to make use of, so do not convey any information via the site map that cannot be obtained elsewhere.

Font, colour and background

Font

The best practice with regard to font style and font and background colours is to allow users control to apply their own preferences (see also Chapter 2, section on 'Computer accessibility using operating system adjustments'). Most modern browsers also provide support for a user's preferences, where a user can set web pages (which have been developed to support users' preferences, not locked into an arbitrary style) to appear in a manner appropriate to their needs. However, the setting of a User Style Sheet can offer more flexibility to choice of preferences. User Style Sheets can be used to override the presentation of HTML-based web pages. They can be extremely powerful in enforcing the way in which the user desires a web page to be presented. Users can set options of text font, size and colour, the font colour of hyperlinks, the linearity of the web page etc. User Style Sheets are a client-side application of Cascading Style Sheets (CSS). Users can also install a range of plug-in toolbars on their browser, which allow them to exert their preferences, but again, only if the page has been constructed in a user-friendly way to allow this.

Obviously, even if users can exert their own preferences and change them, you have to select a font for the website to display in the first instance. There has been much debate regarding the use of serif (e.g. Times New Roman, Rockwell) or sans serif fonts (e.g. Arial, Verdana, Comic Sans). The general consensus (including advice from the British Dyslexia Association[3]) is to use a sans serif font on screen as this increases readability for a majority of users, including a large majority of dyslexic users, although the Royal National Institute of Blind People (RNIB) simply advises the avoidance of fancy or indistinct fonts. The debate on this issue rages on (Poole, 2004).

Debate also continues regarding the minimum size of font that is acceptable on web pages. Many users now concur that anything smaller than 12 point should be avoided, while the RNIB recommends a minimum of 14 point. If a web page is created with relative rather than absolute font sizes, users can amend the font size to suit their needs by adjusting browser settings. Avoid underlining, capitalizing or italicizing large chunks of text, as these can drastically reduce readability. If you wish to distinguish sections of text, for example quotes, indenting them will visually distinguish them without decreasing readability. However, there should also be a notification within the text itself for those unable to see the indentation.

Colour

Use any colours that contrast well with each other but are not so bright as to be distracting, and bear in mind that a large of number of people are red-green colourblind, and other, less well known combinations also occur (e.g. blue-yellow colourblindness). Popular combinations include black/navy with cream/yellow, but any combination is acceptable if the contrast is sufficient - displaying the page in greyscale will help to show if the level of contrast is adequate for readability. Using the Vischeck website[4] will also enable the website designer to see how the page may look to people with colourblindness and related conditions. Because of the fact that some users cannot always distinguish colours, do not use colour alone to convey meaning (for example, 'the items shown in red are no longer available' would not be satisfactory).

Background

Avoid background patterns, images and watermarks where possible - these simply serve to distract the eye, and there are very few users who find them helpful (see Hall and Hanna, 2004).

Images

Text descriptions

'A picture paints a thousand words' - discuss! Images serve so many purposes within web resources that the ways in which they are treated must be judged on a case by case basis. Images are often used to convey information. If this is the case they should carry an audio explanation or a text alternative (in HTML an 'ALT tag' or 'longdesc' for longer pieces of text) that is usable by screen-reading software to describe the information contained within the image to users who cannot see it - also, providing a description in the text can enable users who may not be able to interpret the image or understand its meaning. The text description should convey the meaning of the image, and not simply be a physical description. Leave the alternative text blank (a 'null' ALT tag) if there is no meaning to the image and it is purely for decoration. For example, do blind users need to know that the image on the travel agent website is of 'a happy family playing in a pool'? Does it give them any real information or does it just clutter their browsing experience?

If images are used to show relationships between concepts or ideas (for example a map with clickable regions that each lead to different information) this information also needs to be provided in audio or text format, to allow non-mouse users to make the same choices as mouse users.

Print or hard copy

A further issue to consider is whether your web resource is likely to be printed to hard copy by users. Many images degrade to the point of being meaningless when printed on single-colour printers. This effect can be easily checked, and can avoid users obtaining useless images in their printed copies.

Pixelation

Finally, there is the issue of pixelation. When magnified, some images lose definition and become illegible. This is most often true with images of text (for example, flow charts). It is easy to check whether or not this is the case by using the magnifier supplied within your operating system (e.g. the one located in Windows XP at Start > Programs > Accessibility > Magnifier) or a free one downloaded from the internet (such as that provided by iZoom[5]). It may be necessary to advise users who access your site using screen magnifiers to select the alternative you have provided for an image if this is the case. It is also necessary to bear in mind that users of screen magnifiers may not be able to view the whole of the image at one time. If there is a relationship between parts of the image (again, flow charts provide a good example), this may be rendered inaccessible to screen magnifier users who cannot see the image in its entirety. Again, it may be appropriate to advise them to access the text or audio alternative for that image (see also Chapter 3, section on 'Magnification').

Links

As discussed in the section on navigation earlier in this chapter, it is of value to a range of users to keep the number of links per page to a manageable number. The links themselves should make sense when taken out of context, that is, when read alone without the surrounding text. To speed the navigation of blind users, screen reading programs extract all of the links from a page into a single window. The user can then skim through the links alphabetically and progress quickly through the site to the information required. However, this works only if the links make sense out of context - so 'News' is far more useful than 'List of news headlines', 'More news', 'Click here for more news' or even the dreaded 'Click here'.

If a link is going to take the user to a different site, or open a new window, this should be indicated. There should also be an indication if information is to open in a new format e.g. Microsoft® Word or Adobe® PDF. The more information users can be provided with, the less likely they will be to become lost, frustrated or unable to progress, the antithesis of usability.

Multimedia

Communicating information by multimedia alone is always a risky strategy, as multimedia is often inaccessible to some users in some way, whether related to a particular need of the user or to a technological issue (for example, many open access computers do not have sound cards enabled, or may not have the latest Adobe® Flash player installed). So the best practice with multimedia is always to have information presented in a variety of ways. Multimedia can be very engaging for some learners who do not gain the most from a text-based environment - however, it should not be the only means of conveying information.

Audio and video files

Embedded audio and video files should also have user control. If you cannot see the screen it can be frustrating and unsettling for sound to begin playing outside of your control. Any links to alternate versions should ideally feature before the multimedia in the tabbing order, so users know there is an alternative before they are faced with what they may find to be an inaccessible version. As above, if media content is set to open in a new window, or through a separate player (e.g. Windows Media Player) this needs to be stated before the content is accessed.

Plug-ins

If a user needs to download a plug-in to access multimedia, this should be sensitively handled to enable those who can use the multimedia to obtain the plug-in. The way the multimedia will act should be clearly stated, so users who will not be able to access it do not waste time and effort downloading a plug-in for something they will not be able to access. Many users lack confidence in the use of technology and the concept of downloading plug-ins will make them uneasy, so the process should be explained as clearly as possible. It is also likely that many users (such as those accessing content from a public computer suite) will not have the appropriate administrator rights to download software or plug-ins. This highlights again how an 'accessibility' issue is actually a wider 'usability' issue when taken in the context of the types of users who will access the material.

For further information on making multimedia accessible, see the excellent Skill For Access website.[6]

Alternate versions

The most important consideration with the provision of alternate versions of website features is to ensure that at the end of the process users have all attained the same information and, where relevant, have had equivalent experiences, with a similar degree of ease. An alternate version that does not carry the same information as the original is a second-class service, and is ethically, not to mention legally, unacceptable.

The reason why text-only versions of websites are generally advised against is not that they are bad practice per se, but because they are a cover for bad practice, or at best lazy practice. If the original version of a website is designed inclusively there is no need for a text-only version. Further, a separate text-only version is easy to miss when updating the site (let alone easy to miss as a user, as the links to them can be hidden in the wider page navigation), and hence a text-only page can very easily become a second-class service. The automated tools that transform a regular web page into a text-only version avoid the updating issue, but still do not cater for the full range of needs that the users of your website may have.

Where alternate versions are a worthwhile addition to your site is where audio, visual or other forms of information are an integral and necessary part of your main site and you need to cater for the needs of users who cannot access them. Each instance should be treated individually and in context. In other cases a text version may be the appropriate alternative, in some cases an audio version or a sign language interpretation avatar or video, in some cases captions or a text transcription of audio or video (in which case descriptors are often required in addition to simple transcription of utterances). In each case think of what is required of the user in order to access the information (and gain an equivalence of experience), and how someone who cannot meet that requirement may otherwise be able to receive information (not necessarily always in electronic form) - this should guide you as to the best means of providing an alternative.

Accessibility information

Many sites now carry an 'accessibility statement'. However, the vast majority of these, rather than providing the user with practical information on how to make best use of the site's facilities, instead focus on a corporate statement of the efforts made towards accessibility, sometimes not even focusing on the website but on the organization as a whole! Some do contain helpful user information, but it is buried beneath the corporate statement. In a report for TechDis, Sloan et al. (2006) make several valid recommendations on this theme:

- Every page of your web resource should have a clear and consistent link to the accessibility page.
- Provide helpful information in a task-focused way, giving users the advice

they need in order to use the features within the site or their browser, such as changing font type and size, colours and so on. If bespoke accessibility features are provided (see next section), list them on this page.
- Link to existing good practice advice providing user-led modifications to their browsing experience.

The accessibility page should also include contact information for someone who can provide advice and guidance for users experiencing difficulties in getting what they require from the site. The routes to this resource should also be accessible (see also Phipps et al., 2004).

Bespoke accessibility features

There are a number of accessibility features that can be made available on a website. For example, user preference options can be provided to enable users to change the background and text colour along with text size. It can be very useful to provide users with these options - however, also of use is providing users with the facility to change the settings within their browser as this is a useful tool to know when accessing websites without such options (see also Chapter 2, section on 'Display settings').

Another possible accessibility feature to consider is the use of Access Keys. In general, Access Keys are not considered helpful as there is no consistent advice as to which keys should represent which action - for example, on some sites F3 may take the user to 'Contact us' and on others 'Latest news'. It is highly unlikely that a user will spend enough time on any one website to get to know the Access Keys sufficiently well for them to be much use. If a site's navigation is consistent and easy to understand, then Access Keys should be unnecessary. The exception to this rule is where the site may be returned to again and again by the user, for example a library catalogue. In this instance, having a clear and consistent set of Access Keys may be of benefit to some regular users (see also Chapter 2, section on 'Keyboards').

Conclusions

In order to create a website that is fit for use by all potential users, a process must be undertaken that examines each of the issues identified in this chapter and addresses each of them in the context of the site and its aims and purposes. It may be helpful to consider an overview of this process in the form of a series of questions. These questions should help establish the user type for the website and thus the needs that may need to be catered for.

- What is the purpose of the website? It could be to provide information, deliver a service, act as a gateway, engage the user in interaction, and so on.
- What is the breadth of the audience? Is it the general public or a defined group? If it is a defined group is it a known group? If it is a known group have the users been invited to comment on the kinds of facility they would find useful within the web resource?
- Where is the resource likely to be used? Is it likely that mobile devices will be used to access the resource? Is it likely that users with slow internet connections will need to access the resource?
- What needs are easily within your ability and resource to cater for?
- Where can you go for expert advice on accessibility features that are beyond your capability?
- What alternatives are available for items on your website? What might be possible in addition?
- Who makes the final decision on resourcing - if more resources are required to make your website accessible, is the decision maker aware of the legal responsibilities? (See also Chapter 4, section on 'Legal and policy factors').

There is no definitive right and wrong answer when creating a website, and no checklist or benchmark against which one can accurately and objectively judge accessibility. However, if the website designer understands the purpose of the site and the ways in which it needs to provide sufficient flexibility to meet the needs of the full range of likely users, then a usable site is likely to result. It is hoped this chapter will serve as a tool for that process to be better understood and more widespread in the domain of the information and library professional.

References

Brazier, H. and Jennings, S. (1999) Accessible Website Design, *Library Technology*, 4 (1), February, 10–11.

DRC (Disability Rights Commission) (2006) *Publicly Available Specification 78: guide to good practice in commissioning accessible websites*, www.equalityhumanrights.com/en/publicationsandresources/Disability/Pages/Websiteaccessibilityguidance.aspx.

Hall, R. and Hanna, P. (2004) The Impact of Web Page Text-Background Colour Combinations on Readability, Retention, Aesthetics and Behavioural Intention, *Behaviour and Information Technology*, **23** (3), 183-95.

Newell, A. and Gregor, P. (2001) User Sensitive Inclusive Design, *Interaction Homme/Machine and Assistance*, invited lecture, 4/5/6 July 2001, 18-20.

Olejniczak, B. (2004) Optimising Your Chances with Web Accessibility, *Digital Web Magazine*, http://digital-web.com/articles/optimizing_your_chances_with_accessibility/.

Phipps, L., Harrison, S., Sloan, D. and Willder, B. (2004) Developing and Publicising a Workable Accessibility Strategy, *Ariadne*, **38**, (January), www.ariadne.ac.uk/issue38/phipps/.

Poole, A. (2004) *Literature Review: which are more legible: serif or sans serif typefaces?* www.alexpoole.info/academic/literaturereview.html.

Sloan, D., Dickinson, A., McIlroy, N. and Gibson, L. (2006) *Evaluating the Usability of Online Accessibility Information*, www.techdis.ac.uk/index.php?p=3_10_10_1.

Zeldman, J. (2001) *Taking Your Talent to the Web*, Populi, Inc. ISBN 0735710732.

URLs

1 www.plainenglish.co.uk
2 www.techdis.ac.uk/simdis
3 www.bdadyslexia.org.uk
4 www.vischeck.com
5 www.issist.com
6 www.skillsforaccess.org.uk

Chapter 4

The importance of web accessibility

DAVID SLOAN

Introduction

Web accessibility has in recent years emerged from being a niche area of web development of little general interest to become something of a hot topic, discussed by web developers and designers, a subject for academic research and something that is increasingly influential at a policy, contractual and legislative level. Why should this be? There is, of course, a basic moral argument that people should not face undue discrimination as a result of their disability. This social motivation is one of four core arguments presented by the Web Accessibility Initiative (WAI) of the World Wide Web Consortium (W3C) in its drive to promote online accessibility (W3C, 2005). This chapter looks at the motivations and arguments for accessibility.

Social factors

The most fundamental argument for web accessibility is simply that including people with sensory, physical and/or cognitive disabilities enables access to web resources for a wider proportion of the target audience than would otherwise have been reached.

Disabled people are frequently identified as a group experiencing social exclusion because of barriers they face in attempting to perform everyday tasks such as accessing information or communicating; participating in or receiving services such as entertainment, shopping, education and health-care; and democratic processes such as voting in government elections. The barriers encountered by disabled people may include physical obstacles such as stairs in the built environment, or lack of information in a suitable alternative medium for those with visual or hearing impairments. These real-world accessibility barriers may exist to such an extent that the independence of the disabled person is severely restricted, or even lost.

The world wide web, as conceived by its founder Tim Berners-Lee, was intended as an information and communication space in which participation was not affected by personal circumstance, such as a disability. Berners-Lee foresaw the potential of digital information and web services to overcome many of the challenges faced by disabled people in the physical world (see Chapter 5, section on 'World Wide Web Consortium').

So, for example, by using the web, the *same* electronic information and services provided by a website that has been designed with accessibility in mind can be accessed by:

- people who are blind or visually impaired, who can use text-to-speech devices to listen to the content in audio format, or Braille displays to output the content in tactile format
- people with low vision, who can use screen magnification software to enlarge the text size of the content
- people with dyslexia, who can adjust the appearance of the text, or use colour filters to enhance readability
- people with reduced reading skills, who can use text-to-speech reading software to read aloud specific pieces of text.

The benefits of the web as a single, highly accessible information and communication medium are clear when considering the effort that would be required to create, distribute, maintain and update alternative versions of the same information – for example printed copy in large print, or on different coloured paper, printed as Braille, printed as Easy-read or recorded as spoken audio. With the web, information is made available in one accessible format from one source, and is available to people where and when they need it, in a way that best suits their specific requirements (see also Chapters 2 and 3).

As well as providing accessible information, accessible web design can also ease data *capture* and *manipulation* for people who, because of their disability, may have difficulty using, or be unable to use, paper-based forms, or speech-based systems such as telephone banking. Beyond this, the importance of supporting accessible content *creation* is particularly relevant, as the web evolves into an increasingly egalitarian space where extreme technical skills are no longer essential for people to create and publish content - or even make money by providing online services. The variety of genre in content creation - from personal opinion expressed in a weblog, to sharing images, audio and video via websites such as Flickr, YouTube and MySpace, to storing academic course work through e-portfolios, to designing e-learning resources, to trading in goods through electronic auction sites such as eBay - opens up new possibilities for disabled people to contribute actively rather than passively. Accessible web design can make this happen in a way the physical world cannot (see also Chapter 10, section on 'A look to the future').

Beyond the level of the individual, a corporate or public organization's commitment to social responsibility is increasingly seen as a necessary image to project. Demonstrating a positive approach to inclusiveness may be considered particularly attractive from a publicity perspective - so, if an organization can identify and remove potential accessibility barriers in the web resources it provides, this commitment to web accessibility will be seen as a strong indicator of social responsibility (Waddell, 1999).

Economic factors

Since accessibility, at its most basic level, concerns ensuring that the widest possible range of people can access and use a web resource for its intended purpose, there is a clear potential economic benefit in widening the target audience - or customer base - of a website that offers goods or services to the public.

Arguments outlining the financial benefits that can ensue from a well designed, accessible website have historically been hindered by a lack of concrete data demonstrating the benefits. This situation changed after a presentation by Legal and General, the UK financial services company, at the 2006 launch of a new UK standards document that gives guidance on the process of commissioning accessible websites. Some compelling statistics were presented that showed the financial benefits experienced since the launch of the company's redesigned website, where accessibility had been a core influence on design:

- a saving of £200k per annum on site maintenance
- an increase of 95% in site visitors obtaining an insurance policy quote
- an increase of 90% in sales of online life insurance sales
- a predicted 100% return on investment (ROI) in the redesign project in significantly less than 12 months
- a 30% increase in natural site traffic
- a 5% reduction in page loading time
- effort in site maintenance reduced from an average of 5 days per job to 0.5 days per job.

It might be difficult to specifically demonstrate from these statistics that the improved performance resulted from the improved accessibility of the new Legal and General site, rather than a more general improvement in usability, or any other factor. It would be more difficult, though, to dispute that accessibility was part of a successful project of improvements made to an e-commerce website, resulting in a measurable return on investment. (As an independent validation of its accessibility, the new site was named 'Site of the Month' for January 2007 by members of the Guild of Accessible Web Designers.)

Of course, for many websites, there may be a not-insignificant initial expenditure required to bring the site up to an acceptable level of accessibility; these costs increase with the number of accessibility problems present and the complexity and size of the original resource. Additionally, there is no denying that some accessibility techniques, such as providing synchronized captions and audio description for digital video, bring unavoidable financial and time costs, which may in some circumstances limit their use.

Yet an equivalent situation exists in the physical world, where the costs of improving the accessibility of an old building of complex architecture are likely to be much greater than of a new-build where lifts, wheelchair ramps, easy-open doors and Braille labelling are installed as a fundamental design specification. These features may add slightly to initial costs, but if left out may affect the resale value or even legality of the building. So, while implementing accessibility improvements to a web resource may incur initial costs, the impact of those efforts on site visitors is likely to have a positive long-term cost-benefit for an organization. The goal of accessible design is to make a website available to a wider audience, and while commercial sites such as Legal and General can immediately measure success through increased sales, for public sector sites such as library websites, the demonstrated success of improving accessibility may be better measured in terms of increased visits, in repeat visits or in transactions conducted via the web.

A final consideration, when looking at the economic motivations for web accessibility, is to consider potential cost *savings* that may ensue. In particular, financial benefit may arise from:

- reduced costs in maintaining the website, due to improved efficiency in design; this may lead to more general efficiency improvements within an organization
- avoidance of potentially costly legal action arising from alleged unlawful discrimination against disabled people; and avoidance of the potentially negative financial impact of the publicity surrounding such a case.

Technical factors

Related to the potential economic benefits of web accessibility are a number of technical benefits. One of the most compelling arguments has been the emergence of search engine optimization (SEO) as a key consideration in web design, particularly in the retail sector, where the race to have one's website appear at the top of the results of a web search for a particular product has strongly influenced the architecture and design of websites.

There are many parallels between effective (and ethical!) search engine optimization and accessible design, illustrated by the list of tips provided by Google to help web authors make sure their pages are successfully indexed by the search engine (Henry, 2006). This stems from the similarities between the way the indexing software used by the Google search engine retrieves and indexes web content and the way screen reading technology used by blind people operates - for example, neither can 'see' graphics, but both can access any text alternative provided for a graphic.

Beyond the parallels with search engine optimization, there are a number of other technical benefits of accessible design, each of which may in turn lead to cost savings over time:

1 Accessible web design techniques tend to promote more efficient presentation of online information, optimizing navigability and thus making sites easier to use. This can be marked by a resulting decrease

in load on the server hosting the website, as there are fewer unnecessary page requests by users struggling to find the information they need.

2 Accessible design promotes a separation of content - i.e. information and functionality - from appearance, through technologies such as Cascading Style Sheets. This means that the maintenance work required either to add to or change content, or to change appearance, should be relatively straightforward, without introducing additional complications.

3 Accessible design also encourages the use of design techniques, standards and technologies that promote interoperability across diverse browsing environments, whether these are older browsers of limited functionality or emerging browsing platforms. In theory, this means that as new browsing technologies come on stream, there should be minimal work required to ensure that the site works well for them.

Legal and policy factors

While many accessibility advocates prefer to highlight the benefits that an accessible website can realize, organizations also need to be mindful of any legal responsibilities they may have to ensure they do not unfairly discriminate against disabled people. In many countries around the world legislation exists that either directly or indirectly puts responsibility on organizations that provide services through websites to take action to ensure as far as possible that disabled people can access those services.

Note that the advice presented in this section is a lay interpretation of legislation as it existed in April 2007. Readers are strongly recommended to seek independent legal advice for clarification of the relevant legal situation in their own country.

Legislation in the UK

Disability Discrimination Act 1995

In the UK, the Disability Discrimination Act 1995 (DDA, 1995) sets out the rights of disabled people not to encounter unjustified discrimination on account of their disability. The DDA, under its constituent parts, places obligations on:

- employers who employ disabled staff (Part II)
- organizations that provide the public with goods, facilities and services (Part III)

- organizations that provide post-16 education (Part IV). Part IV of the DDA was introduced in 2001 by the Special Educational Needs and Disability Act (popularly known as SENDA).

From the above list, it is clear that most large organizations will have obligations under the DDA on a number of different levels.

The question of how the DDA relates specifically to websites has been one of some debate. Where the web and, more generally, ICT are concerned, the DDA legislation does *not* specifically state what is and is not required in order for an ICT to be 'legally accessible'. Reference is made to websites in the DDA's accompanying Codes of Practice. (While being legal documents, these are not actual legislation, rather examples of where the legislation does and does not apply, and what is and is not lawful practice.) It is generally accepted that the DDA would apply to a service provided by a website (see Sloan, 2001 for an overview from a legal perspective), but as yet no case law exists in the UK, no court decision having been made on this.

Some see this situation as a weakness in the legislation, in that it makes objective assessment of a legally accessible website impossible. From a positive angle, though, the DDA does allow organizations to use ICT, including websites, in the best possible way, so as to help them meet their obligations under the DDA. It also means that, since there is - at the time of writing - no legal definition of a 'DDA-compliant' website, there is also no legal definition of a 'DDA *non*-compliant' website. So, organizations have some scope to use the web in a creative way to improve the accessibility of the services they provide, while also having a duty to ensure that their web resources do not introduce unjustified barriers for disabled people. Under the DDA, it is therefore reasonable to assume that the use of a web resource by a service provider in which certain services are inaccessible to some disabled people is not unlawful, so long as:

- the accessibility barriers are justifiable
- the service provider has taken reasonable steps to provide access to the inaccessible services in another way.

The first condition does not excuse poor web design - for example failing to follow recognized accessible web design guidelines. The DDA does, however, allow justification of accessibility barriers on, for example, technical or financial grounds, or the grounds of preserving academic quality.

The 'Disability Equality Duty' (DDA, 2005)

In 2005 the DDA was extended to introduce the Disability Equality Duty (DED). The DED applies specifically to public organizations in the UK, and extends the requirements set out by the DDA that organizations promote equality for disabled people. The DED requires organizations to develop and publish a Disability Equality Scheme, a plan of action for improving equality. In addition to specific aims for improving accessibility, the plan should demonstrate how the organization has consulted disabled people in formulating its plans for improving equality, and also should set out how the organization will gather - and publish - evidence of progress towards meeting the objectives of the DED.

A detailed description of the DDA legislation is beyond the scope of this chapter - for more information readers are referred to:

- the website of HMSO[1] for the legislation text
- the website of the Equality and Human Rights Commission[2] for the DDA Codes of Practice and other supplementary information.

Copyright (Visually Impaired Persons) Act 2002

The Copyright (Visually Impaired Persons) Act 2002 was introduced to overcome a problem whereby restrictions placed on copying printed and other information subject to the Copyright, Designs and Patents Act 1988 also prevented the creation of accessible alternative versions of the copyrighted material.

The Act permits the copying, without permission, of copyrighted material if the reason is to improve the accessibility of that material for a person meeting the Act's definitions of a visually impaired person or physically impaired people. It also defines what sort of material is covered by the Act, and defines the extent to which material may be copied and distributed.

Legislation elsewhere

Legislation outlawing disability discrimination exists in many other countries - legislation that either directly or indirectly applies to web accessibility (Waddell, 2006). In the USA, the Americans with Disabilities Act (ADA) enshrines the basic rights of disabled citizens not to encounter unjustified discrimination in a similar way to the UK's DDA. Additionally, Section 508 of the Rehabilitation Act directly addresses accessibility-related issues of technology, by requiring federal agencies to procure and provide only technology that meets accessibility standards referred to in the legislation.

In Australia, the Disability Discrimination Act (DDA) was introduced in 1992, and is the legislation on which the UK's legislation of the same name is based. Australia's DDA is historic in web accessibility circles, in that it featured in the first-ever successful legal action taken by a disabled person against a provider of an inaccessible website. In 2000, Australia's Human Rights and Equal Opportunities Commission found that the Sydney Organising Committee of the Olympic Games had breached the DDA by failing to provide information on its website in a form that a blind person could access. Since that time, this ruling has, understandably, been influential in raising awareness of the importance of web accessibility.

Other countries that have introduced legislation that directly or indirectly mandates web accessibility, or references standards relating to web design, include Canada, Denmark, Germany, Israel, Italy, Portugal and Spain. The European Commission additionally has issued a resolution encouraging member states to address the issue of web accessibility as a matter of urgency.

The W3C provides an updated list of national web accessibility legislation and policy.[3]

Barriers to adoption of web accessibility

Any discussion of the motivations for considering web accessibility should also look at counter-arguments or obstacles to promoting accessible design, particularly when introducing a policy of accessibility in a large organization. After all, why is it that, despite apparently compelling reasons for making websites as accessible as possible, the reality is that accessibility levels are routinely found by surveys to be 'disappointingly low' (81% of UK sites failing to meet a basic level of accessibility, according to a 2004 Disability Rights Commission survey)?

A number of factors have been suggested as reasons for this apparent lethargy in improving accessibility of the web as a whole. These issues reflect the wider challenge that faces the movement promoting Design for All (also known as Universal Design or Inclusive Design - see Chapter 3, section on

'What is 'Design for All'?'), which attempts to persuade manufacturers of consumer products as well as communication and information technology to ensure the needs of disabled people are accommodated during the design process. Inclusive design advocacy projects such as i-Design in the UK (Keates and Clarkson, 2004) and the Universal Design Research Project in the US (Vanderheiden and Tobias, 2000) have investigated attitudes in industry towards accessibility and inclusive design, and identified some key barriers to uptake.

Cost of accessible design

One main obstacle to uptake of inclusive design is the perception that it is simply too difficult and expensive, despite the potential rewards outlined earlier in this chapter. In part, this reflects industry's cautious approach to anything that might be seen as excessive investment (for example, adding accessibility features) for unjustifiably low returns (a very small increase in customer base - those disabled people benefiting from the accessibility features added).

Many accessibility advocates have argued that this need not be the case, but there is also an acceptance that the way accessibility is described, particularly if it is implied that it ensures 'universal' access to 'everyone', can lead to problems:

> The concept Design for All is misleading . . . it gives to the designers the idea of a highly sophisticated and not cost-effective design process by which their products will reach a wider hypothetical market (the strength of which) has not been shown to them. (Velasco and Verelst, 1999)

Accessibility and creativity

Another common barrier, particularly in the product design industry, arises from the stereotyping of inclusive design and accessibility as 'designing for the institutionalized'. In other words, some designers may believe that accessibility leads to the creation of products that look obviously as if they had been designed for a small minority, and are therefore expected to have little attraction for the rest of the market. In the web design field, this is reflected in the perception that accessible websites can only be achieved when aesthetic appeal and functionality are compromised (Zeldman, 2003).

Turning this on its head, some accessibility advocates have criticized web designers and developers for failing to use technology in an imaginative and creative way to enhance accessibility of information, services and experiences (Slatin, 2002). This could be argued to be an effect of a guideline-based approach to design, where accessibility is perceived - incorrectly - as a list of non-negotiable 'dos and don'ts'.

It is true that some accessibility design guidelines may seem to restrict practice, but as a colleague of the author neatly summed up the issue: 'without some form of constraint [for example, commercial sensibilities or legal obligations], design becomes art' (personal communication). After all, in the car manufacturing industry, certain design standards are almost universally preserved (for example, the use of a steering wheel to control direction, or the arrangement and operation of clutch, brake and accelerator), yet the view that this stifles creativity in automobile design is rarely heard!

Even so, there is an ongoing challenge in demonstrating that web accessibility can allow for beautiful, exciting and useful websites that users will wish to use, return to and recommend others to visit. The Web Standards movement[4] has led the way in attempting to show that the two objectives can be achieved together. This has in turn spawned initiatives such as the CSS Zen Garden,[5] which showcases examples of how the same basic web page can give unique and visually stunning designs through the use of Cascading Style Sheets, and the Guild of Accessible Web Designers (GAWDS).[6] GAWDS runs a Site of the Month competition, with the aim of rewarding sites for both visual design and accessibility; the Accessites website[7] has similar goals of showcasing examples of websites that have been peer reviewed against accessibility and design criteria.

Lack of legislative clarity

A third reason cited for lack of adoption of accessibility in web design is a lack of clarity over legal responsibility, and this was demonstrated in the findings of two recent surveys of attitudes towards accessibility, by Lazar, Dudley-Sponaugle and Greenridge (2004) and Milliman (2002). For some organizations, it seems only the threat of legal action may be powerful enough to force a change in practice, and even then only doing just enough to avoid legal action may be seen as necessary. The lack of technical direction over what is and is not required, and a lack of case law, is enough for some organizations to dismiss the issue as being of no importance.

Alternatively, they may decide 'doing nothing' is worth the risk if expenditure on fixing accessibility problems is estimated to be more than the likely financial penalty a breach of the law would incur. This contrasts with situations where the very fear of potential legal action may be enough for others to spend time and effort in improving the accessibility of their website - or to panic and overreact, removing potentially valuable web-based material on the assumption that it may be unlawfully discriminatory.

In some countries, the rights of disabled people not to encounter discrimination are not as yet specifically protected by law, meaning there is no legal mandate for web developers in these countries to consider accessibility. While there are calls for tighter, clearer legislation, the impact of case law remains unclear, particularly in the USA, where cases brought under the Americans with Disability Act (ADA) have not always resulted in a judgment in favour of web accessibility advocates. Legal obligations as a motivator for accessibility are therefore not always as influential as they might be - hence the preference of many accessibility advocates to promote the benefits of accessible websites rather than to warn of legal responsibilities.

Where there has been a noticeable positive impact of legislation on inclusive design and web accessibility it has come about when the legislation has impacted on market trends (Vanderheiden and Tobias, 2000; Keates and Clarkson, 2004). Rather than 'push' legislation that requires industry to act by threatening a punishment for non-compliance, 'pull' legislation seeks to promote accessibility by influencing markets through mandating the *purchasing* of accessible products.

The best example of this is in the USA, where Section 508 of the Rehabilitation Act requires US federal agencies to procure and provide accessible technology but, critically, does not require industry to produce it. Of course, the effect is that organizations that want to sell to financially very powerful federal clients rush to ensure their products meet the requirements of Section 508, and it is surely no coincidence that many commercial web technologies have significantly improved their support for accessibility since Section 508 came into force. The happy outcome is that these improvements have been felt globally, even though the legislation that arguably did most to instigate the improvements applies only in the USA.

Lack of organizational support

Finally, a major stumbling block cited by advocates of accessible design within large organizations, and also identified in surveys of attitudes towards accessibility, is a lack of wider awareness of or support for accessibility within the organization. Implementation of an effective accessibility policy at organizational level cannot be achieved by enthusiastic individuals working in isolation. Yet this is, anecdotally, the typical situation in organizations, often made worse when the 'accessibility champion' leaves the organization or is redeployed to a position that has less direct influence on accessibility issues.

Contributions and support are required from all who have responsibility for material published online, from web developers and designers to sales and marketing, legal affairs, IT departments, and - crucially - senior management. To be effective, an accessibility strategy must cover both web resources produced internally and those commissioned from third parties.

Urban and Burks (2006) and the WebAIM project (WebAIM, 2003) have both recognized the importance of a collaborative approach to implementing a successful accessibility policy, and identified essential elements of an organizational accessibility strategy as including:

- securing commitment from senior management
- establishing an accessibility body with clearly defined goals and responsibilities for overseeing accessibility, comprising representatives from across the organization, and headed by an accessibility champion
- identifying the current state of play with respect to accessible online content
- developing a plan for improving accessibility, with goals and a timeline; this should cover training and support frameworks as well as actual development tasks to be carried out; the plan should also specify a definition of 'accessible', and how, when, and by whom that condition may be assessed
- monitoring progress, including creating a policy for incentivizing accessibility - rewards for successes and a consideration of what happens to resources (and those responsible for them) that fail to meet the defined level of accessibility within the defined time.

(See also Chapter 7, section on 'Accessibility policies'.)

Summary

The benefits of accessibility can be summarized as:

- Accessible websites promote social inclusion for disabled people by improving access to information, communication and services.
- Accessible websites can bring financial benefit, both by increasing potential customer base and providing savings in maintenance of the site.
- Accessible websites can result in technical benefits, such as enhanced visibility to search engines, and increased usability in general.
- Legal obligations exist in many countries that require organizations to ensure that accessibility barriers do not lead to discrimination against disabled people when accessing online services.

Effective adoption of accessibility as an organizational strategy involves persuading stakeholders that the approach can lead to financial benefit, that visual appeal and functionality do not have to be sacrificed, and that accessibility requires a collaborative effort. Relying on a single individual to deal with accessibility will be doomed to failure.

References

Copyright (Visually Impaired Persons) Act 2002, London, TSO, www.opsi.gov.uk/acts/acts2002/20020033.htm.

DDA (1995) *Disability Discrimination Act 1995* (c. 50), London, TSO, www.opsi.gov.uk/acts/acts1995/Ukpga_19950050_en_1.htm.

DDA (2005) *Disability Discrimination Act 2005* (c. 13), London, TSO, www.opsi.gov.uk/ACTS/acts2005/20050013.htm.

DRC (Disability Rights Commission) (2004) *The Web: access and inclusion for disabled people*, London, TSO, www.equalityhumanrights.com/en/publicationsandresources/Disability/Pages/Websiteaccessibilityguidance.aspx.

Henry, S. (2006) Understanding Web Accessibility. In Thatcher, J. et al. (eds), *Web Accessibility: web standards and regulatory compliance*, Friends of Ed.

Keates, S. and Clarkson, J. (2004) *Countering Design Exclusion – an introduction to inclusive design*, London, Springer Verlag.

Lazar, J., Dudley-Sponaugle, A. and Greenidge, K. (2004) Improving Web Accessibility: a study of webmaster perceptions, *Computers and Human Behavior*, **20** (2), 269–88.

Milliman, R. (2002) Website Accessibility and the Private Sector: disability stakeholders cannot tolerate 2% access!, *Information Technology and Disabilities*, **VIII**, www.rit.edu/~easi/itd/itdv08n2/milliman.htm.

Slatin, J. (2002) The Imagination Gap: making web-based instructional resources accessible to students and colleagues with disabilities, *Currents in Electronic Literacy*, **6** (Spring), www.cwrl.utexas.edu/currents/spring02/slatin.html.

Sloan, M. (2001) Web Accessibility and the DDA, *Journal of Information, Law and Technology (JILT)*, 2, www2.warwick.ac.uk/fac/soc/law/elj/jilt/2001_2/sloan.

Urban, M. and Burks, M. (2006) Implementing Accessibility in the Enterprise. In Thatcher, J. et al. (eds), *Web Accessibility: web standards and regulatory compliance*, Friends of Ed.

Vanderheiden, G. and Tobias, J. (2000) *Universal Design of Consumer Products: current industry practice and perceptions*, http://trace.wisc.edu/docs/ud_consumer_products_hfes2000/index.htm.

Velasco, C. and Verelst, T. (1999) Raising Awareness Among Designers of Accessibility Issues. In de Baenst-Vandenbroucke, A. (ed.), *Proceedings of INTERACT'99 Workshop: making designers aware of existing guidelines for accessibility (Edinburgh, 1999).*

W3C (2005) *Developing a Web Accessibility Business Case for Your Organization: overview*, World Wide Web Consortium (W3C), www.w3.org/WAI/bcase/Overview.

Waddell, C. (1999) *The Growing Digital Divide in Access for People with Disabilities: overcoming barriers to participation in the digital economy*, www.icdri.org/CynthiaW/the_digital_divide.htm.

Waddell, C. (2006) Worldwide Accessibility Laws and Policies. In Thatcher, J. et al. (eds), *Web Accessibility: web standards and regulatory compliance*, Friends of Ed.

WebAIM (2003) *An 8-Step Web Accessibility Implementation Model*, www.webaim.org/coordination/implementation/.

Zeldman, J. (2003) *Designing with Web Standards*, Indianapolis, Indiana, New Riders.

URLs

1 www.opsi.gov.uk

2 www.equalityhumanrights.com/en/Pages/default.aspx

3 www.w3.org/WAI/Policy
4 www.webstandards.org
5 www.csszengarden.com
6 www.gawds.org
7 www.accessites.org

Chapter 5

Accessibility advice and guidance

JULIE HOWELL

Introduction

Web developers and website owners have been confused by the apparent array of web accessibility guidelines available on the web. Those web developers who have received formal training in web design and development may have touched upon accessibility only briefly during their studies, if at all. Website owners may have heard about the importance of web accessibility through the media or may have been informed by their legal, human resources or strategy departments that their organization is now subject to a legal duty to provide web-based services that disabled people can use.

Awareness in the public and private sectors

Civil servants who work in the public sector are likely to know more about accessibility, as there has been greater responsibility placed upon them by way of legislation to ensure that all citizens can access their web-based services. At the other extreme, small businesses are perhaps less likely either to be aware of the importance of accessibility or to have created sites that are usable by disabled people (owing to lack of appropriate resources).

Those information professionals working in the public sector are therefore most likely to be aware of the need to ensure that their organization's website is accessible. Those working in medium-to-large private companies will probably be aware that they have a legal duty, although they may be unsure of how this duty might be met. Those working in small businesses and voluntary organizations (apart from those directly connected with disability issues) are least exposed to the messages about accessible web design, and are therefore likely to be the most in need of help (of course, there are exceptions).

The information professional's responsibility

It may be argued that information professionals have a responsibility within their organization to ensure that information about the importance of web accessibility reaches both those with management responsibility for the organization's website and those directly responsible for the technical construction and editorial content of the site. The Disability Discrimination Act 1995 (DDA, 1995) places a legal duty on employers to ensure that employees are not subject to disability discrimination. A corporate website that cannot be used by a company's own disabled employees may be in breach of the DDA. Therefore companies and organizations arguably have a dual role to ensure their websites are accessible to any disabled employees (current or future) as well as external customers (the public or other businesses) (see also Chapter 4, section on 'Legal and policy factors').

Web accessibility: a history

In the early 1990s the web offered a very reasonable level of accessibility to disabled people. In those first few years, the web was largely text only. The software used by disabled people to read websites worked very effectively on well ordered, text-rich sites. However, from around 1996 the situation began to change. Websites became more graphical. Developments in Hypertext Mark-up Language (HTML) made it possible to design web pages that were more visually appealing. This did not make websites any less accessible to disabled people. The access technology that they used - such as the screenreader software used by blind people - continued to interpret the HTML and transform the code into audible, synthetic speech that was easy to follow when you relied on hearing to read the screen.

The impact of web content authoring tools

It was the arrival of automated web content creation software ('authoring tools') that first signalled a negative impact on disabled people's experience of the web. Up until this point, anyone designing a website had to learn to 'hand code' HTML. This necessity had a fortunate by-product: it encouraged the creation of what we now describe as 'standards-conformant code'. Until the arrival of authoring tools, many people learned how to create websites by following HTML tutorials in books, magazines and on the web. While it is true that hand-coding can be laborious and time consuming it at least meant that websites were coded 'correctly'. Authoring tool developers sought to make the process of creating web pages easier, and so web authoring software with graphical user interfaces was developed that hid from view the HTML coding. Creating a link or styling a heading became an exercise in pointing and clicking. Unsurprisingly, authoring tools quickly became the most popular way to create websites and soon a nation of web developers who knew very little about structured HTML was creating the majority of web content.

More graphics

As developers' hunger for greater graphical capabilities increased, so authoring tools crept further and further away from the ideal of strict HTML-conformant coding. Tools were engineered to create web pages that looked exactly how the user of the tool wanted them to look, regardless of the underlying code. The result was a generation of websites that looked great on screen (though often different in different browsers and at different screen resolutions). However, these sites were often reduced to incoherent nonsense when accessed by a blind person using a screenreader.

The age of the inaccessible web had dawned.

Browsers move away from web standards

During the late 1990s, browser developers also took a step away from standards. Web browsers became notoriously 'forgiving' of non-conformant web code, even when code fell some way short of the original standard expected for a website to render correctly through a browser. Now browsers would still display websites as the author intended, even when the underlying code was poor. This gave developers further disincentive to code correctly, and so standards-compliant, accessible coding became the exception rather than the norm.

The World Wide Web Consortium

Professor Sir Tim Berners-Lee, inventor of the web, is chairman of the World

Wide Web Consortium (W3C). W3C 'develops interoperable technologies (specifications, guidelines, software, and tools) to lead the web to its full potential'.[1]

Berners-Lee has said, 'The power of the web is in its universality. Access by everyone, regardless of disability, is an essential aspect.' When it became clear that large numbers of disabled people now found themselves effectively locked out of the web, Berners-Lee created a project group of the W3C – the Web Accessibility Initiative (WAI). WAI 'works with organizations around the world to develop strategies, guidelines, and resources to help make the web accessible to people with disabilities'.

Berners-Lee tasked WAI with creating recommendations on the creation of accessible web content. Since 1999, WAI has produced three sets of guidelines. When these are implemented in harmony across the web, a more accessible web-browsing experience for everyone will be realized.

The Web Accessibility Initiative guidelines

WAI publishes three sets of web accessibility guidelines. This is a fact – arguably – less well-known than it should be. WAI takes the view that only when all three sets are in use universally can the ultimate goal of a more accessible web be achieved:

- Web Content Accessibility Guidelines (WCAG)
- Authoring Tool Accessibility Guidelines (ATAG)
- User Agent Accessibility Guidelines (UUAG).

Web Content Accessibility Guidelines (WCAG 1.0)

The most widely discussed and publicized of the three-part set of WAI guidelines is the Web Content Accessibility Guidelines (described hereafter as WCAG 1.0).

WCAG 1.0 was published in May 1999. The purpose of WCAG 1.0 is to guide website developers in the development of website content that is universally accessible.

WCAG 1.0 comprises 14 guidelines (or principles) grouped into three conformance levels according to priority as follows:

- Priority 1: A web content developer *must* satisfy this checkpoint. Otherwise, one or more groups will find it *impossible* to access information in the document. Satisfying this checkpoint is a basic requirement for some groups to be able to use web documents.

- Priority 2: A web content developer *should* satisfy this checkpoint. Otherwise, one or more groups will find it *difficult* to access information in the document. Satisfying this checkpoint will remove significant barriers to accessing web documents.
- Priority 3: A web content developer *may* address this checkpoint. Otherwise, one or more groups will find it *somewhat difficult* to access information in the document. Satisfying this checkpoint will improve access to web documents.

Each of the 14 guidelines is supported by one or more checkpoints (there are 64 checkpoints in total):

- When a developer is satisfied that the content s/he has designed meets all 16 of the Priority 1 checkpoints then s/he may claim the site meets WAI WCAG 1.0 Level A.
- When a developer is satisfied that the content s/he has designed meets all of the Priority 1 and 2 checkpoints (there are a further 30 checkpoints at Priority 2) then s/he may claim the site meets WAI WCAG 1.0 Level AA.
- When a developer is satisfied that the content s/he has designed meets all of the Priority 1, 2 and 3 checkpoints (there are a further 18 checkpoints at Priority 3) then s/he may claim the site meets WAI WCAG 1.0 Level AAA.

Developers are entitled to display an appropriate WAI conformance level logo on their site when they are satisfied their content meets the checkpoints for that priority level.

However, this system of self-certification has been found to be unreliable for a number of reasons:

1. It has been argued that a WCAG 1.0 conformant website is not necessarily usable by disabled people. Developers who claim conformance without also involving disabled people in testing their site may discover that they meet the specified criteria for one of the WAI WCAG 1.0 logos and yet their site is not usable by disabled people and therefore may

be in breach of disability discrimination law.

2 Every page on the site, and every element of every page, must meet all the checkpoints in the chosen priority level. Many sites that claim conformance have been found to contain pages deeper within the site that fail to meet all the necessary checkpoints.
3 It has been argued, most notably by the Disability Rights Commission (in its 2004 report *The Web: access and inclusion for disabled people*), that many sites that conform to WCAG 1.0 priority levels 1, 2 or 3 are very difficult for disabled people to use (more information about this later in this chapter). (DRC, 2004)

Some organizations, including the Royal National Institute of Blind People (RNIB),[2] AbilityNet[3] and the Shaw Trust,[4] offer accessibility audits and certification based on WCAG 1.0 that include user testing by disabled people. This mix of automated testing, user testing and conformance with WCAG 1.0 is sometimes referred to as 'real world accessibility'.

In their paper 'Contextual Web Accessibility', Kelly and Sloan (2006), make a very strong argument for use of WCAG 1.0 as one component of an accessibility toolkit, suggesting that 'context' is of great importance when making judgements on how to apply the WCAG (see Kelly and Sloan, 2006, and Chapter 10, section on 'Building on the WAI approach').

Detailed information about WCAG 1.0, including the guidelines themselves and technical documentation that support their use, is available at the W3C website.[5]

Critics of WCAG 1.0 express concern that the guidelines are too prescriptive, while others have complained that they are too vague.

At the time of writing, WCAG 2.0 is in development. However, as further changes are likely to be made to these guidelines prior to their becoming a WAI recommendation it would be unwise to discuss their content here. Up-to-date information about WCAG 2.0 is available at W3C website[6] (see also Chapter 10, section on 'The role of WCAG 2.0').

Authoring Tool Accessibility Guidelines (ATAG 1.0)

According to WAI, 'authoring tools are software and services that people use to produce web pages and web content'. Examples include commercial web authoring tools such as Microsoft's FrontPage and Adobe's DreamWeaver, content management systems (CMS) and tools that author different types of web content such as PDF or Flash.

While there has been much effort on the part of web accessibility advocates to encourage web developers to implement WCAG 1.0, it must also be acknowledged that lobbying every person who creates web content would be a monumental, and probably impossible, task. In the mid-1990s, most web developers coded sites by hand. By the beginning of this century, most developers were using authoring tools of the type described above to create websites. Coding by hand is still an important skill, especially when bug-fixing is required, but authoring tools make web design quicker and easier.

The advent of authoring tools means that anyone can be a web developer. On the one hand, this is a welcome development as it means that anyone can create a website and express themselves via the web. On the other hand, it means that fewer and fewer web developers understand the importance of web standards (such as the WAI guidelines) and that many appear far more concerned about how their site 'looks' than about its interoperability or accessibility.

Web developers' pre-occupation with the visual appeal of their sites really wouldn't matter if the authoring tools they use created web standards-compliant code. The problem is that they don't. In fact, very few of the tools available on today's market produce accessible, standards-compliant code by default. Therefore, it has become easier to create an inaccessible website than an accessible one.

The developers of authoring tools are under constant pressure to deliver products that produce great-looking sites. Unfortunately, accessibility comes much further down the tool developers' wish list. As web developers' are the ones buying the authoring tools it continues to be important that accessibility campaigners lobby web developers to purchase authoring tools that create accessible code.

At the same time, authoring tool developers are being lobbied to adhere to WAI's Authoring Tool Accessibility Guidelines (ATAG 1.0). Detailed information about ATAG 1.0, including the guidelines themselves and technical documentation that support their use, is available from the WAI website.[7]

User-generated content

In the latter half of the first decade of the new millennium there has been an explosion in a phenomenon known as 'user generated content'. In previous years, anyone could make their voice heard in cyberspace by setting up their own website. Now, this is no longer necessary. Blogs are quickly replacing personal websites as a means for individuals to air their point of view. Rather than creating a blog site from scratch, a number of 'blogging tools' are available and web users simply use their templates, code and hosting facilities. Blogging tools are web authoring tools in just the same way as FrontPage or DreamWeaver. Other tools that enable web users to be web developers without any understanding of web code include photo-sharing sites such as Flickr,[8] social networking sites such as MySpace[9] and wikis such as Wikipedia[10] (see also Chapter 10, section on 'A look to the future').

Therefore it is vital that the companies that develop sites that enable web users to create web content ensure their tools author accessible code. Authoring tool developers should also ensure that their tools are usable by disabled people - in many countries, including the UK, this is a legal requirement under disability discrimination legislation.

Because few web developers now hand-code content and more rely on authoring tools, we are moving into a time when ATAG 1.0 will be more crucial to disabled people's access to the web than WCAG 1.0. Already, a number of the major authoring tool developers are working with WAI in the development of ATAG and related resources (e.g. Microsoft, Adobe, IBM, Apple).

The goal must surely be for all authoring tools to create accessible code with very little effort or intervention on the part of the web developer. Put another way, authoring tools should make it impossible for web developers to create inaccessible code. At present, accessibility tends to be an option that is not set as a default and can easily be switched off. In some cases, the onus to switch on the accessibility checks is placed on the web developer, as these features are buried deeply within the authoring tool, with accessibility scarcely mentioned in any help screens or supporting documentation. While this remains the case, web developers must be reminded of why accessibility is so important and the consequences of locking disabled people out.

Legal incentives to accessibility

In the USA a piece of legislation known as Section 508 of the Rehabilitation Act places a legal duty on the Federal Government to procure software that creates accessible output and is usable by disabled people. As the federal government is the largest purchaser of IT in the USA, Section 508[11] has provided authoring tool developers with a strong incentive to make changes to their software of the type described above. There is no similar legislation in Europe at present, although the EU is considering the introduction of such over the course of the next few years. Further information is available on the European Disability Forum website.[12]

It is very important to note that under present UK legislation software developers do not have a legal duty to ensure the accessibility of their tools. Until this situation changes, information professionals must perform their own checks when selecting authoring tools. For example, ask the vendor to what extent their product conforms to ATAG 1.0. Without legislation, it is unlikely that authoring tools will become fully accessible in the near future, unless customers are prepared to demand that accessibility be built into the products. Software companies are likely to respond to consumer pressure. As the legal duty to create accessible web content rests with service providers, information professionals must be aware that they cannot place the burden of blame for inaccessible content on the shoulders of the software developer when their purchasing decision is really at the heart of the problem. Information professionals may find it appropriate to seek legal advice on this point when procuring web authoring software in volume, lest a very costly, avoidable and difficult-to-rectify mistake be made at this stage.

User Agent Accessibility Guidelines (UUAG 1.0)

According to WAI,[13] 'user agents' are 'Web browsers, media players, and assistive technologies'. In essence, any software that presents web content in a manner that the user can read is a user agent.

In the case of disabled people, screenreaders (as used by blind people) and speech recognition software are popular user agents. Browsers, in their various types and versions, are also user agents, and it's important to remember that disabled people often adapt their browser settings, thus negating the need for an additional user agent such as screen magnification software.

UAAG 1.0 is for the developers of browsers, media players and assistive technologies and ensures that the user agent can read WCAG-conformant code.

UAAG 1.0 is the essential final piece in the three-part set of WAI guidelines. Without it, all effort to create WCAG 1.0-conformant code is wasted. How a user agent interprets and presents code is essential to disabled people's ability to access that web content.

The developers of browsers and other user agents are engaged with WAI to develop UAAG. However, few user agents fully conform to UAAG as yet.

Detailed information about UUAG 1.0, including the guidelines themselves and technical documentation that support their use, is available from the WAI website.[13]

Publicly Available Specification 78 (PAS 78)

Publicly Available Specification 78: guide to good practice in commissioning accessible websites (PAS 78) was commissioned following a Disability Rights Commission (DRC) report that exposed very poor levels of accessibility among UK business and public sector websites.

The report, published in 2004 under the title *The Web: access and inclusion for disabled people* (DRC, 2004), revealed that 81% of the 1000 websites tested fail to meet Level A of the Web Accessibility Initiative (WAI) Web Content Accessibility Guidelines (WCAG). WCAG Level A contains the fundamental accessibility criteria that every website should meet as a bare minimum.

On learning that so many websites fail disabled people, the DRC commissioned the British Standards Institution (BSI) to produce new guidance for website commissioners (i.e. business and public sector organizations). The 2004 research indicates that while there is much goodwill towards disabled web users, there is almost universal failure to provide websites that disabled people can use. DRC identified a gap between goodwill and good practice that might be bridged by additional guidance on the process of procuring accessible websites.

Julie Howell (then of RNIB, now with digital design agency Fortune Cookie) is technical author of PAS 78 and wrote the first draft. The document was redrafted by an expert industry panel that included IBM, Tesco.com, the Cabinet Office, the Usability Professionals Association and the BBC. Following redrafting, PAS 78 was reviewed by 120 interested parties from around the industry, who returned 188 pages of comments. The document was redrafted a final time and PAS 78 was published in March 2006.

PAS 78 has a shelf-life not exceeding two years. Its future will be reviewed in March 2008.

It is important to understand that PAS 78 does not seek to replace the

WAI guidance that you have read about elsewhere in this chapter. WCAG are technical guidelines. PAS 78 suggests a process for applying WCAG to greatest effect, for achieving maximum usability by disabled people and for meeting the legal duty that has been placed upon service providers by the Disability Discrimination Act (since 1999).

PAS 78 directs website owners to the importance of coding to web standards. The appropriate standards are listed, as is a checklist for appointing an agency to carry out the work.

The document stresses the crucial importance of involving disabled people in user testing of a site before it goes live, and guidance on how to do this is included. The DRC report of 2004 reveals that automated testing cannot uncover all of the access issues a disabled person may find, and lists testing with disabled participants as a key recommendation.

PAS 78 introduces two key concepts that will be new ideas for many site developers and owners:

1. That an 'accessibility policy' be written (for internal use) that identifies the segments of the audience the business or organization is trying to reach and how the design will meet the needs of this diverse audience (as 10–15% of the population has a disability, all service providers must consider disabled people among their target demographic).
2. That an 'accessibility statement' be posted on the website for disabled people to read that details the extent to which the site is accessible, with any exceptions. An invitation to disabled people to provide feedback should be available and any queries or comments from disabled people should be prioritized for action.

PAS 78 is available from the EHRC website.[14]

Usability by disabled people

Accessibility is often misunderstood as the practice of ensuring that disabled people can use the web. In practice however, accessibility is the ability of any person (regardless of disability) using any technology in any circumstance to access (or reach) the content on a website.

It is important to distinguish between 'accessibility' and 'usability'. Accessibility ensures users can reach the content on a site but is no guarantee they will be able to find what they are looking for easily or complete a transaction in a reasonable amount of time. Usability, however, ensures that users are able to complete tasks successfully.

Usability by disabled people is therefore the designer's goal: where a disabled person can complete a task at the same time, in the same time, at the same cost and at the same convenience as users who don't have disabilities.

The research undertaken by the DRC (2004) proved that websites that conform to WCAG 1.0, and score well when measured by automated accessibility checkers, are not necessarily usable by disabled people. As automated tools are unable to measure conformance to all WCAG 1.0 checkpoints (for example, a tool can detect alternative text but cannot tell if the text alternative is useful to a disabled person), testing with real people is essential.

UK Disability Discrimination Act 1995 and web design

Web developers often confuse conformance to WAI's guidance with compliance with UK disability discrimination law.

The question 'how should I design my website to make it conformant to the Disability Discrimination Act' has no clear answer at present. However, it is abundantly clear that the owners of publicly accessible websites have a legal duty to make their online services usable by disabled people.

It is more helpful to think of conformance with the DDA in terms of how usable a disabled person might find a website. A website may be considered usable if a disabled person can complete a task:

- at the same time
- in the same time
- at the same cost and
- at the same convenience

as someone who is not disabled.

This would seem to be a recipe for equality, which is what the DDA seeks to ensure (see also Chapter 4, section on 'Legal and policy issues').

Technical accessibility certainly has a role to play in ensuring equality, but is just one element of a process of ensuring the usability of a website by disabled people.

Keeping up to date

In the absence of county court case law, it is impossible to say what constitutes a 'DDA conformant' website. However, with the DRC and the BSI backing the document, it is likely that PAS 78 is the best guide to meeting your legal duty to disabled web users until such time as case law is established.

Version 1.0 of the WAI Web Content Accessibility Guidelines was published in May 1999. Version 2.0 of WCAG has been in development for a number of years but at the time of writing a launch date has yet to be announced. WAI advises that until version 2.0 is published as a WAI recommendation, web developers should continue to adopt version 1.0. Although version 1.0 requires updating the guidance remains 'stable', whereas the draft of version 2.0 is subject to change. Therefore, developers may read version 2.0 with interest, but should be very wary of following any draft recommendation, lest the guidance should change prior to publication.

PAS 78, like all publicly available specifications published by BSI, is due for review after two years. In the case of PAS 78, review is due in March 2008. PAS 78 was commissioned by the DRC. However, during 2007, the DRC was disbanded and has been replaced by a single equalities commission that is also concerned with matters of race and gender equality: the Equality and Human Rights Commission (EHRC).[15] Commissioners at EHRC must decide whether to commission a review or revision of PAS 78. Possible outcomes of a review include a redrafting or further development of the specification into a full British Standard. Information about the status of PAS 78 post-March 2008 will be available from BSI or the EHRC.

Accessibility lobbyists continue to put pressure on software developers to ensure their products conform to WAI ATAG. When developing content with the aid of an authoring tool, developers should consult the documentation supplied by the software company, which should describe the extent to which accessible content is created by the tool. The large software companies, including Microsoft and Adobe, should continue to publish guidance on their websites that directs users of their authoring tools on how to create accessible content.

Campaigning organizations, such as the RNIB and Abilitynet continue to publish information about web accessibility on their respective websites.

An EU initiative is developing a harmonized methodology for assessing accessibility. Outputs of this project have included a Unified Web Evaluation

Methodology (UWEM 1.0), published in July 2006 (see also Chapter 9, section on 'Web accessibility benchmarking').

At the time of writing, a Google search on the term 'web accessibility' returned some 10 million results. However, developers should check the source of any accessibility guidance for credibility. The WAI guidelines and PAS 78 are the definitive guides to creating accessible online content. The WAI website and PAS 78 provide references to other credible sources of information about accessible web design. Any guidance that deviates from WCAG should be applied with great care.

A large number of web design agencies and consultancies have jumped on the accessibility bandwagon and offer many accessibility services, from design and build to auditing and accreditation. Lest money be spent inappropriately, it is vital to check the credentials of companies that claim to create accessible content or audit for accessibility. RNIB, Abilitynet and the Shaw Trust offer accreditation services based on the WAI standards. Any agencies that claim to produce 'DDA-compliant' sites should be treated with a degree of suspicion, as until DDA case law has been established it is impossible to know how to make a website DDA compliant.

Conclusion

Over the past decade, the range and depth of information about accessible web design has grown and matured. In particular, the recommendations published by WAI (WCAG) and DRC and BSI (PAS 78), and guidance published by individual software developers (Microsoft, Adobe, Apple, IBM), provide a rich, comprehensive and credible source of information. Independent agencies such as RNIB, Abilitynet and the Shaw Trust provide accreditation services based on the WAI and PAS 78 guidance.

Web technologies are constantly developing. For accessibility to be ensured now and into the future, those bodies that set the standards for web content creation must be encouraged to keep accessibility at the forefront of their thinking. Accessibility is difficult and expensive to retrofit. When considered at the very beginning of the standards-setting process, and at the earliest stages of the website and software design lifecycles, accessibility can be a core component that ensures the widest possible audience will enjoy the web today and into the future. A rich source of information, standards and guidance is the Tiresias website.[16] The site is maintained by Dr John Gill, Chief Scientist at RNIB, who regularly updates the site with relevant publications and guidelines.

Information professionals should be aware that British and international standards, and guidelines such as those produced by WAI, are almost always subject to a period of public consultation. Consultations provide the opportunity to shape the guidance. This can be very important if the panel drafting the guidance does not represent the information profession. Information professionals often have direct contact with end-users and so their input into standards and guidelines development can be crucial. To be kept up to date with relevant standards that are in production, it is advisable to contact BSI.[17]

References

DRC (Disability Rights Commission) (2004) *The Web: access and inclusion for disabled people*, London, TSO, www.equalityhumanrights.com/en/publicationsandresources/Disability/Pages/Websiteaccessibilityguidance.aspx.

Kelly, B. and Sloan, D. (2006) *Contextual Web Accessibility: maximising the benefits of accessibility guidelines*, www.w4a.info/2006/presentations/18-David-Sloan-et-al.pdf.

URLs

1 www.w3.org
2 www.rnib.org.uk
3 www.abilitynet.org.uk
4 www.shaw-trust.org.uk
5 www.w3.org/wai
6 www.w3.org/wai
7 www.w3.org/wai
8 www.flickr.com
9 www.myspace.com
10 www.wikipedia.org
11 www.section508.gov
12 www.edf-feph.org
13 www.w3.org/wai
14 www.equalityhumanrights.com/en/publicationsandresources/Disability/Pages/Websiteaccessibilityguidance.aspx
15 www.equalityhumanrights.com/en/Pages/default.aspx

16 www.tiresias.org
17 www.bsi-global.com

Chapter 6

Accessibility evaluation and assessment

DAVID SLOAN

Introduction

Evaluating the accessibility of a website is an important part of accessible web design, whether as part of a new design project, or an assessment of an existing resource for potential barriers. While the goal of an accessibility evaluation or audit is simple – to identify any barrier that may limit or prevent a disabled person from using the subject website for its intended purpose – the diversity of user needs, browsing set-ups and functionality provided by web resources can make evaluation complex and challenging. Thankfully, there are many tools and techniques that can help people without significant accessibility expertise and experts alike to identify where accessibility problems may exist in a website.

Finding the problems is only half the story, though, as there is also the matter of acting on the results of the evaluation. In other words, how can we use the evaluation findings to help improve the accessibility of the resource in question? This chapter looks at effective techniques for evaluating a website's accessibility, and how these can best be presented in a way that helps those responsible for removing or reducing the barriers identified.

Evaluation aims

The immediate aim of a website accessibility evaluation should be to uncover all *true* instances of where a disabled person may have difficulty using or be unable to use the site for its intended purpose and to avoid reporting instances of barriers that do not actually adversely affect accessibility. Results are particularly likely to be relevant if the evaluation looks at the accessibility of the tasks supported by the website, rather than individual pages. This more holistic approach focuses on how users will be interacting with the site, which in most cases will be a flow through a series of pages rather than visiting pages in isolation (Kelly, Phipps and Swift, 2004) (See also section on 'Building on the WAI approach' in Chapter 10).

The status of the website under review may influence what evaluation techniques are used, and how the results are reported. Ideally, an accessibility evaluation will take place early on in the design and development of a website, and will be repeated periodically as things evolve. Early prototypes can be assessed for potential accessibility problems, and any necessary adjustments made as soon as possible, so that when the resource is formally evaluated closer to its release, there should, in theory, be little chance of new, significant barriers being discovered that require major changes to the design.

In reality, though, the likelihood is that an accessibility review will be conducted of a website that is already live, or is shortly due to be published, having been developed in-house or by a third party, and where previously accessibility may not have been a high-profile consideration. The evaluation may be required in order to confirm that contractual obligations towards accessibility have been met by a third-party developer, or that internal accessibility standards have been met; or the organization behind the site may only recently have realized its obligations to optimize the accessibility of the site. Unfortunately, there may be little time available for the evaluation to be carried out, reducing the likelihood that all problems will be identified. Of those problems that are identified, the lateness of the accessibility evaluation in terms of the site's lifecycle, especially if the resource has been live for some time, means that these problems may be significant barriers, and may not be easy to rectify.

Therefore one of the most important aspects of an accessibility evaluation is the need for accurate reporting of problems, and for appropriate prioritization of barriers in terms of where solutions are most urgently required.

Evaluation techniques

The subject of web accessibility evaluation has, in recent years, attracted a sizeable level of attention, both as a practical challenge and as an academic research topic. This has been marked by a recent flurry of activity in developing methodologies and techniques for assessing accessibility, and in the production of specific tools to support evaluation (see also section on 'Web accessibility benchmarking' in Chapter 9).

Web accessibility evaluation techniques can be categorized into one of three distinct groups:

- automated code inspections
- manual accessibility inspection techniques
- user evaluations.

Each group varies in terms of:

- type and number of accessibility barriers found
- reliability of results: does the evaluation technique accurately identify the impact of the barriers found? Or will the barriers identified in reality have a greater or lesser impact on disabled users than the evaluation might imply?
- expertise and technical resources required to conduct the evaluation and interpret the results
- time, effort and financial expenditure required to arrange and conduct the evaluation.

Automated code inspections

Automated tools can greatly help in the task of accessibility evaluation by inspecting the underlying HTML code for potential accessibility barriers. These tools can be set to access a web page, set of pages or entire website, and analyse the HTML code against a set of accessible design criteria, which are typically selected checkpoints of the WCAG. The results of this analysis will normally be presented as a report, in varying levels of detail, identifying for each page the location and nature of accessibility issues found. Some tools can present the results in graphical form, for example by showing the analysed page, adding icons to indicate the location of potential problems.

Table 6.1 lists some popular automated accessibility evaluation tools. In addition, while not specifically accessibility focused, the following free automated tools from the W3C can analyse pages, providing useful accessibility information:

- W3C Markup Validation Service (an HTML checker)[1]
- W3C CSS Validation Service[2]
- W3C Link Checker.[3]

Table 6.1 Automated accessibility tools

Tool	Provider	Type of tool	Web address	Free of charge?
Accessibility Checker	ATRC, University of Toronto; TRACE Center, University of Wisconsin	Online form Downloadable source code	checker.atrc.utoronto.ca	Yes
A-Prompt	ATRC, University of Toronto; TRACE Center, University of Wisconsin	Downloadable software	www.aprompt.ca	Yes (though support has been discon-tinued as ATRC devotes attention to the Accessibility Checker)
Cynthia Says	HiSoftware	Online form	www.cynthiasays.com	Yes
Functional Accessibility Evaluator	University of Illinois	Online form	fae.cita.uiuc.edu	Yes
TAW	Fundacion CTIC	Online form Browser extension Downloadable software	www.tawdis.net	Yes
The WAVE	WebAIM project and Temple University	Online form Browser extension	www.wave.webaim.org	Yes
WebXact	Watchfire	Online form	webxact.watchfire.com/	Yes
AccVerify	HiSoftware	Downloadable software	www.hisoftware.com/access/newvIndex.html	No
Bobby	Watchfire	Downloadable software	www.watchfire.com/products/webxm/bobby.aspx	No
Lift*	UsableNet	Online form Downloadable software	www.usablenet.com/products_services/products_services.html	No

* The Lift series of products includes Lift Online, Lift Machine and Lift for Adobe DreamWeaver.

Attractions of automated tools

There are a number of attractions for the use of automated tools for accessibility evaluation (Thatcher, 2006; Sloan et al., 2002):

- Automated evaluation tools allow fast reporting of accessibility problems without requiring human intervention.
- Automated tools are extremely well suited to performing the often very repetitive task of code inspection and analysis more accurately and effectively than a human.
- Using an automated tool does not require the levels of accessibility expertise that other assessment methods may demand.
- Automated tools can be particularly useful for rapid generation of data that can be used to benchmark a website against accepted best practice; or for comparison between sites, or of a single site's accessibility over time.

Drawbacks of automated tools

There are also, however, several shortcomings of relying on automated tools for accessibility evaluation (Thatcher, 2006; Vanderdonckt and Beirekdar, 2005; Englefield et al., 2005; Spindler, 2002; Brajnik, 2004; Thompson, Burgstahler and Comden, 2003; Diaper and Worman, 2003; Faulkner and Arch, 2003; Ivory and Hearst, 2001). The most fundamental issue is that any automated tool can identify only accessibility barriers that do not require human detection and judgement, meaning that even after a tool is used to evaluate a web page, many of the most potentially significant accessibility barriers remain undetected. This limitation is, to be fair, generally made clear in the documentation of the tools listed in Table 6.1, but may easily be missed or ignored by someone quickly looking to evaluate a web page without true regard for the goals of an accessibility evaluation. Other shortcomings include:

- Automated tools cannot satisfactorily use contextual information to accurately report the real impact of any barriers they find.
- Automated tools may report false negatives (fail to identify accessibility barriers that are present in a web page) or false positives (report errors that are not in fact accessibility barriers); this can lead to variations in how different tools, and versions of the same tool, will assess the same page.
- The reports produced by some automated tools can be long, complex and overly technical, presenting information in a way that makes it difficult to extract the key information necessary to make repairs to the evaluated website.

The final issue relating to automated tools lies in their ease of use. For many people, particularly those without the time or inclination to become familiar with the complexities of web accessibility, an automated tool would appear to support workflow by quickly providing useful and accurate statistical data on accessibility, making comparison and reporting easy and effective. Used in this way, the educational value of such tools in prompting additional manual checks is lost, and instead the tool output is presented as an authoritative, yet unvalidated and possibly inaccurate, quantitative measure of the site's accessibility. Sadly, this can lead to overestimates of a site's accessibility, resulting in a site that is considered 'accessible', even though many disabled people will struggle to use it as intended.

Manual accessibility inspection

Manual accessibility evaluation methods typically involve an evaluator inspecting pages of the website, identifying potential barriers as they go. With manual techniques, the quality of data gathered can be extremely high, and the process of converting findings to specific design changes can be extremely efficient, particularly if the evaluation process can be combined with the repair process, by making changes to the site and reassessing whether a barrier still remains.

Inevitably, this requires a degree of expertise in accessible design, in order to have an awareness of potential issues and how to spot them. Manually checking a very large website can also take a significant amount of time. The job has, however, been made easier by the development of accessibility guidelines - most notably the W3C's Web Content Accessibility Guidelines, which can be used as a reference to guide the evaluation (see also secton on 'Accessibility advice and guidance' in Chapter 5). An effective manual inspection should not, however, be seen simply as a checklist type of exercise. For best results, it should involve viewing pages under a variety of browsing conditions, which in some cases may require changes to browser settings, or viewing in different browsers or using tools to simulate specific browsing situations.

Manual inspection processes

It is generally recommended that a manual inspection should include:

- Viewing the site with images turned off: does the site still make sense?

Have appropriate alternatives been provided for graphical content?
- Viewing the site with browser text size increased: can all text still be read? Does all text actually change size?
- Viewing the site with style sheets turned off, and/or when an alternative style sheet is applied. Does the site still make sense?
- Viewing the site in black and white: does any information rely on the ability to detect colour?
- Viewing the site in a small or very large browser window: how does this affect page layout? What level of scrolling is required to view page content?
- Viewing the site with JavaScript turned off: is there information or functionality that cannot be accessed without support for scripting?
- Browsing the site without using the mouse: are there any instances of content or functionality that cannot be accessed without using a mouse?

Areas where specific attention should be paid include:

- quality of written content: in particular spelling and grammar; and the general appropriateness of the language used for the target audience
- presentation of content: for example the use of headings, short paragraphs and lists to present textual content
- the use of multimedia, and the presence of accessibility features such as captions and audio description
- the presence of animated content, particularly flashing or flickering content, and the extent to which animated content is controllable by the user
- the navigability of forms used for data input, including site search facilities.

Tools for manual inspections

Many of the checks above can be carried out using a standard browser; it is possible to make changes to the browser to simulate some of the conditions above. Usefully, browser toolbars have been developed for popular browsers, bringing together a number of useful accessibility checking tools. Freely available are the AIS Accessibility Toolbar for Internet Explorer[4] and the Web Developer's Toolbar for Mozilla/Firefox,[5] and these toolbars can greatly ease the process of manual accessibility checking through the facilities they provide. They also integrate some of the automated tools described in the section in this chapter on 'Automated code inspections'.

While checking a website under different browsers and on different operating systems is generally considered good practice, the Lynx text-only browser [6] is particularly useful for checking the quality of pages, not so much because it is widely used, but because of its usefulness as a testing tool. For example, Lynx removes formatting such as colour, tables and columns, presenting pages as plain text; as Lynx does not support JavaScript, it can also be used to check for scripting issues.

Lynx can also be a useful indicator as to the quality of experience that a screen reader user will have when accessing the subject site: a crude approximation of a screenreader would be to ask a colleague to read aloud a web page as displayed in Lynx. For an enhanced audio experience, some free text-to-speech systems exist, while many commercial screenreader manufacturers offer free, limited use demonstration versions of their products. Each can be useful for checking the quality of a website when spoken aloud. Generally, though, without dedicated familiarization with a screenreader, it is recommended that for best results screenreader usability be measured by evaluating the site with visually impaired people.

Tools also exist to allow simulation of, or a measure of the quality of, the output of web pages as might be experienced by someone with a specific impairment:

- The Vischeck website [7] simulates the appearance of a site when viewed by someone with a particular colour deficit, by redisplaying a page with colours altered.
- The Colour Contrast Analyser [8] is extremely useful as an aid for checking potential issues in the contrast between text and background colours, allows comparison of the hue and brightness levels of text and background colour pairs, and uses an algorithm to test whether contrast levels are appropriate.
- The Juicy Studio Readability Test [9] can analyse the text of a web page for readability levels against recognized reading level algorithms.

Some checks can be performed by extremely rudimentary means. For example, printing pages out in black and white is a useful check for any colour reliance issues that may cause problems for some visually impaired people, as well as checking the 'print accessibility' of the page. For a right-handed evaluator, using the mouse with the left hand can identify potentially intricate mouse manoeuvres that may be problematic for someone with a tremor or other condition that reduces manual dexterity.

While some organizations may wish to make a significant financial investment in setting up a comprehensive accessibility 'testing station', most of the tools and techniques described above require no additional expense beyond what already exists on a typical desktop computer, making manual accessibility inspection highly cost effective.

Pitfalls of manual inspections

Manual inspections can be very effective, but there are potential problems if focus concentrates too much on guideline conformance. The aim of an accessibility review should be to identify barriers that prevent equitable access for disabled people, but if this is diverted to 'achieving compliance with a set of guidelines', then issues experienced by some people may be neglected, or inappropriately addressed. As a warning of the perils of misinterpretation, Jim Thatcher describes in very effective terms an example of 'how not to do accessibility', a website that appeared to have followed accessibility guidelines but was in practice unusable by anyone using a screenreader (Thatcher, 2003).

Beyond the potential for misinterpretation, there is the issue of the quality of the guidelines themselves. The advice presented in guidelines can lose meaning and appropriateness over time, particularly as web technologies and assistive technologies evolve, so an evaluation against these guidelines may not be the best way of measuring accessibility. In an investigation of museum websites in the UK, some websites were found to have a high level of conformance to the W3C WCAG, yet were also found to be 'unusable by disabled people' (Petrie, King and Weisen, 2005).

The lesson is that manual inspection methods should always go beyond a simple checklist approach, and explore issues that may emerge under a variety of browsing situations.

User evaluations with disabled people

The most effective means of evaluating a web resource for accessibility is to involve disabled people, preferably representative of the target audience. This becomes effectively a usability evaluation, where evaluators are asked to perform a set of tasks that a user of the resource might reasonably be expected to complete when using that resource. An observer takes notes of any problems, as well as details of the accessibility solution(s) used by the evaluators to overcome or minimize the impact of their disability or disabilities.

The particular strength of this method is in its obvious involvement of 'real people', particularly if the disabled evaluators are representative of the subject resource's target audience. So long as the evaluation is task-focused, rather than an invitation to browse the site with no particular goal, the quality of the results found is likely to be extremely high in terms of their validity as genuine problems that potential disabled users of the resource are likely to encounter. This helps to reinforce the message that accessibility is ultimately a socio-technological issue, rather than a purely technical issue that may be addressed by rewriting code based on design guidelines without any need for end-user involvement.

Gathering user evaluation data

In user evaluations, both qualitative and quantitative data can be gathered and used to define improvements required, and also to measure progress made following adjustments made to the site:

- Examples of quantitative metrics might include number of errors, pauses, requests for help, time taken to complete a task.
- Examples of qualitative data gathered might include user comments, gestures or expressions (such as sighs or smiles!) made during tasks, or issues explored further through discussion after the evaluation has been completed.

Audio- or video-recording sessions (with the evaluator's permission, of course) can help to capture issues that might otherwise be missed. In addition, footage of an evaluator struggling with a particular aspect of the site can be a particularly powerful, persuasive and effective way of demonstrating to site developers the problems users can face when using the site.

An added bonus is that where evaluators are using assistive technology, such as a screenreader or alternative input device, or makes an accessibility adjustment to the way the site appears using the browser or operating system, usability observations can also identify the success with which the interface supports access using these technologies or adjustments.

By looking at the evaluation data gathered, the location of accessibility barriers can be pinpointed and assessed in terms of their impact on the user; did a particular barrier stop a user from completing a task, or cause them to abandon using the site? Or did the user manage to cope, or even sail past without noticing the supposed barrier?

This information can be particularly useful for prioritizing which issues should be addressed immediately and which are of less urgency.

Practical issues

Inevitably, though, there are also factors that can make user evaluations with disabled people challenging to arrange, carry out and interpret. Practical issues identified by Petrie et al. (2006); Mankoff et al. (2005); Clark (2003); Coyne and Nielsen (2001); and Newell and Gregor (2000) include:

1. Recruitment challenges: The time required to recruit a pool of evaluators covering a suitable range of impairments can be challenging. Often, organizations may find it difficult to find enough people to form a representative cross section of impairments, and may have to seek users through third parties, such as disability charities or specialist accessibility evaluation organizations, or make do with only a few disabled evaluators.
2. Location of the evaluation: Allied to the general problems of finding sufficient evaluators, specific access requirements, whether technical or physical, may require an evaluation to be carried out at a user's home or office. For example, if an organization expects to conduct evaluations at its premises, the accessibility of the location may make it extremely difficult or impossible for some disabled evaluators to reach. Additionally, it may not be possible to provide the appropriate assistive technology away from an evaluator's own computer, and if they are forced to use an unfamiliar assistive technology, this may negatively bias the evaluation findings.
3. Recompensing evaluators: Attracting evaluators may require some form of inducement, but offering financial reward can be problematic for disabled people receiving financial support from the state, and who may put at risk their eligibility for support if they receive payment for an evaluation.

4 Impact of individual differences: As with any user evaluation, individual differences within a specific group of people, in this case those who share a common disability, mean that one person's experiences may not reflect the population as a whole. Issues such as an individual's general technical expertise, experience with web browsing or familiarity with their assistive technology can influence their interaction with the subject website. An evaluator's physical and mental well-being, which may vary from day to day, or change over the course of a day, may also affect their ability to complete tasks, or their tolerance of any accessibility issues encountered. Some researchers in the field of technology design for older and disabled people have observed a trend whereby evaluators may provide more favourable feedback than reflects their actual browsing experiences, seemingly for fear of disappointing the people conducting the evaluation (Waller et al., 2005; Eisma et al., 2004).
5 Analysis time: Analysis of the results may also take more time than for other evaluation methods, since data capture has to be pooled and analysed after the event, as opposed to directly during the evaluation. The richness of the evaluation data gathered is a benefit of the evaluation method, but inevitably will also extend the analysis process.

The Information Technology Technical Assistance and Training Center (ITTATC) at the Georgia Institute of Technology provides some useful and practical advice on involving disabled people in the design and analysis phase of product development (Georgia Tech Research Corporation, 2004). Additionally, a number of specialist usability and accessibility companies now exist, which can help organizations looking for support in conducting user evaluations with disabled people. Such companies can take care of recruitment and of conducting evaluations, and may also advise on, or take responsibility for, the evaluation design and analysis.

Remote user testing

Remote user testing has been shown to yield valuable data. Here, a disabled person is sent the address of the website to be reviewed, along with a list of tasks to perform. They are asked to carry out the evaluation on their own, recording and returning the results when completed. This can overcome some recruitment challenges and widen the pool of potential evaluators, but the main shortcoming is the loss of an independent observer of the evaluator interacting with the site. As a result, the quality of the evaluation results is dependent on the quantity of information received, and specifically the accuracy with which the evaluator reports their success in performing the tasks, and the problems found.

It may be possible to improve data capture for remote user testing through screen and input capturing software, which can record some additional data on the steps taken for each task, but there is then the issue of installing this (often expensive) software on each remote evaluator's computer. There is also the possibility that evaluators who are willing and able to conduct evaluations remotely are likely to be technically more capable than a 'typical' user, and results may thus be overly optimistic.

Despite these issues, the attractiveness of remote user testing has been such that a number of networks now exist, such as the Usability Exchange,[10] which can put organizations wishing to have their websites evaluated in touch with disabled people willing to act as evaluators.

Hybrid evaluation methods

Given the variations in the accessibility evaluation methods, there is widespread agreement that a hybrid method offers the best balance in terms of resources required and range and quality of results found. Many of the techniques described above are complementary, particularly those that allow for evaluation against a definition of best practice in accessible design, such as the W3C WCAG.

Based on methods promoted by the W3C WAI and others (e.g. W3C, 2005; DRC, 2004; Clark, 2003; Slatin and Rush, 2002; Sloan et al., 2002), Table 6.2 (on p. 86) represents a suggested hybrid accessibility evaluation methodology, which can be adapted if necessary to suit the resources and expertise available to an organization or individual wishing to assess a website's accessibility.

Table 6.2 Hybrid accessibility evaluation methodology

Evaluation stage	Scope
Examine pages using graphical browsers under different conditions: • Images turned off • Text size enlarged using the browser • Style sheets turned off • Scripts turned off • Keyboard only • Monochrome • High and low screen resolutions	As many site pages as possible; but at least the following: • Home page • Selection of pages likely to be frequently visited by users • Page with a form • Page with a table of data • Page with multimedia content
Manual inspection of selected pages using WCAG checklist	
Examine pages using a variety of browsers (including text-to-speech and text only)	
Read and evaluate page content	
Validate HTML of selected pages, and validate CSS	
Run an automated accessibility checker across the website	All pages of the site
User evaluations with disabled people	As many pages as required to complete selection of tasks a site user would typically be expected to complete

New developments in evaluation

Individual differences in evaluation approaches, subjective interpretation of results mean that it can be difficult to achieve unanimous agreement that a website is 'accessible' or 'not accessible'. This has led to a perceived need, at a political level, to define some standard method of assessing accessibility, so that there can be an indication that a resource has been objectively and adequately assessed for accessibility. This has influenced attempts to formalize a series of individual evaluation techniques into a multi-stage method. For example, in Europe, this has culminated in work funded by the European Commission to create a Unified Web Accessibility Evaluation Methodology (UWEM).[11] It includes advice on:

- defining the scope of the website to be evaluated, including sampling of pages
- procedures for automated and manual evaluation of conformance against the W3C WCAG
- aggregation of results from the various evaluation stages
- scoring and reporting of results.

Some researchers have expanded the concept of accessibility evaluation to include more of a usability focus, borrowing techniques from the field of human computer interaction (HCI). This may include a heuristic evaluation where, independently, evaluators assess the website using a set of heuristics, or rules of thumb (Nielsen, 1994). Researchers at IBM produced a set of accessibility heuristics (Paddison and Englefield, 2003), but found that significant expertise was required to apply them in a meaningful way. The Accessibility Walkthrough has been suggested as an alternative evaluation method that requires less expertise, and is more likely to identify real barriers (Brajnik, 2005).

Conducting an accessibility audit

Where an accessibility evaluation is being carried out as an audit, by a team separate from those who maintain the site, it is necessary to ensure that the audit is as useful as possible to the team who will have to act on the results - and anyone else responsible for the quality of the subject website. This means taking appropriate steps both before the evaluation starts and in reporting results.

Advance steps

The nature of an accessibility audit is such that potentially awkward scenarios may emerge, particularly if the review finds significant problems with the site. Without due care, this may read as a relentless criticism of the website development team's skills, or may imply it is wilfully practising discriminatory behaviour. Of course, an accessibility audit should act as a motivational activity to support the development team in its job, and so advance consultation between the accessibility audit team and the people commissioning the audit is highly recommended. This allows objectives to be agreed, so that when the results of the audit are presented, they are likely to be welcomed as useful feedback by those who have to act on them, rather than received with suspicion or hostility as an uninvited attack on a developer's skills or attitude.

Advance communication should involve a request for information about the site, including:

- agreement as to the scope of the accessibility audit
- the intended aims of the site
- intended target audience

- a list of typical tasks that the target audience may reasonably be expected to complete using the site.

Technical information useful to know in advance includes details of:

- the authoring tools that were or are used to create and maintain the site and its content
- the number of people likely to be maintaining the site or adding and editing content
- any reliance on specific non-HTML formats to present content
- any content provided by a third party, the nature of which is beyond the control of the development team.

With this information in hand, an audit can be carried out that is sympathetic to the aims of the site and the circumstances under which it was created and is currently maintained. This gives the best possible chance that the findings presented will be directly relevant to the site, and also pragmatic.

Reporting the audit results

A critical goal of the accessibility audit of a website must be to accurately and effectively communicate the results such that whoever is responsible for improving the site's accessibility can actually make the changes in the most effective way. This means making sure that the accessibility audit not only provides clear advice on what barriers exist and how they can be overcome, but also gives information on how this repair work can best be implemented.

The need to prioritize accessibility issues is particularly important where limited time and resources are available to make changes; while the priorities allocated to each checkpoint of the W3C WCAG can be useful, the frequency, nature and location of an accessibility barrier can make it more, or less, of a problem than its WCAG priority may imply. There is also a danger that without appropriate prioritization, attention will focus only on issues with relatively simple solutions, while issues requiring more complex, but eminently achievable, solutions may be ignored.

The reporting of an accessibility audit should therefore include clear recommendations for improving the site's accessibility, prioritized according to the likely impact of each barrier found on the site's accessibility to disabled people.

Recommendations can be grouped as follows:

- recommendations that should be followed as soon as possible
- recommendations that should be followed if at all possible, but are of less significance than the higher priority tasks, or may require significant effort to implement
- examples of good practice that should be continued. Listing site features that positively enhance accessibility helps to ensure that these are not inadvertently removed, as well as being a generally useful motivational tool.

Each recommendation should describe the work required to address the barrier; additionally, the following information can be helpful:

- a justification as to why the recommendation should be applied - including identifying those users who would benefit from the improvement
- example(s) of where the recommendation should be applied
- any examples of where the recommendation has already been followed in the site.

Recommendations should also be supported by a recovery strategy; advice on which pages should receive attention first. Generally, a pragmatic approach to repairs is recommended, where important pages are attended to first, in particular the home page, and all pages that a user must visit en route to completing key tasks supported by the site. Less frequently visited pages can be amended afterwards (Nielsen, 1999).

The audit report

Beyond a report on accessibility problems and a recommended course of action for overcoming them, the accessibility audit has an arguably undervalued role as an educational and motivational tool. In other words, an effective accessibility audit report will lead readers of all levels of technical ability to a greater understanding of web accessibility and of the ways in which disabled people access the web and the problems they encounter.

Often, when accessibility is discussed in purely technical terms, the repair work emerging from an accessibility audit can seem as a list of fixes to be made to the code, and the underlying rationale behind each issue is lost. While in the short term this may help to ensure that essential fixes are applied as quickly as possible, the lack of context around each fix, why it is being recommended and for whom, makes it likely that the same mistakes will be made a second time. This perpetuates what some see as a gulf between a technical understanding of accessible design and a more holistic appreciation of the diverse browsing environments and challenges that disabled web users face.

When the audit document extends beyond a list of code fixes to provide readers, whether developers, managers or anyone else with an interest in or responsibility for the site, a flavour of the real world experiences relating to accessibility issues, then there is a chance that readers will gain a greater understanding of the problems that exist, and how to avoid them in future. The use of text narratives of user evaluations, or presentation of images or video of the impact of a particular accessibility issue, can help readers to experience what Helen Petrie and colleagues termed the 'Eureka moment' of accessibility (Petrie et al., 2006). They describe this as the point where the act of web developers observing disabled people having difficulty using a website crystallized their knowledge of accessibility from a technical, abstract issue into a genuine appreciation of the problems accessible design tries to address.

Report structure

So, unless it is known precisely who will be reading and acting upon the evaluation results, the audit document should, ideally, be written for multiple audiences with a range of technical and management skills. As such, a suggested structure for an accessibility audit report is:

1 Background and aims: An overview of the importance of web accessibility, highlighting the benefits arising from designing with accessibility in mind and providing an overview of the relevant legal obligations. The report should reinforce that the evaluation was conducted with the aim of helping the developers maximize accessibility rather than as a deficiency report, unless of course the aim of the evaluation is simply to list accessibility issues present in a site as a confirmation that it needs to be replaced.
2 Evaluation findings: For each of the evaluation stages applied, a brief

description of the evaluation method and a narrative description of the findings.

3 Recommendations: Description of each recommendation, with supporting information as listed in the section in this chapter on 'Reporting the audit results', plus advice on an appropriate recovery strategy. It may also be beneficial to provide a summary list of recommendations, in order of priority.

(See also the section on 'Auditing accessibility' in Chapter 7).

Outsourcing an accessibility audit

Frequently the printed and online press and the academic literature will publish the results of 'uninvited' accessibility surveys for research or benchmarking purposes. In fact, public organizations such as libraries, museums and universities may find themselves subject to an accessibility study, which typically finds results 'disappointing'. Sadly, while such studies may be useful publicity for the cause of web accessibility, the results rarely find their way to the site owners in any meaningful form, and, with a few exceptions, the evaluation method is rarely disclosed.

However, there are many very well equipped organizations, in industry, academia and the charity sector, which can provide website owners with expert accessibility audits of their sites, and provide support for removing any accessibility issues that may exist. Organizations that are considering commissioning an accessibility audit of their site would be advised to check the credentials of candidate accessibility auditors, in terms of their track record and previous clients, as well as the quality of the review methodology used. If at all possible, make sure that the audit will include the results of a usability test with disabled people, and ensure that the accessibility audit programme includes a follow-up review to check the quality of any repair work made following the first audit.

Summary

Accessibility evaluation is an essential step in accessible web design. Ideally, it should be an early and regular step in an ongoing web development project; more realistically, it is likely to be conducted on an already live website, or on a site shortly to be published, where many barriers may exist and where there is little scope to make comprehensive changes. Nevertheless, the true value of the evaluation is less in finding accessibility barriers, but more in its success in making the necessary changes happen.

The most effective accessibility evaluation approach is to apply a hybrid of automated and manual assessments, and user evaluations with disabled people. Accessibility guidelines, particularly W3C WCAG, provide an important reference point for an evaluation, but there is also a need to take a more holistic view of accessibility by considering the tasks that the site will support, and to evaluate the accessibility of those tasks, rather than concentrating on individual pages.

In reporting the results of an accessibility evaluation, particularly where the results of the evaluation will be passed on to others for action, it is necessary to make clear:

- what action is required
- why it is required
- the importance of the action required.

At the same time, the value of the evaluation or audit report is that it is a way of raising awareness of accessibility and encouraging a deeper understanding of the issues that will help to ensure that all those who read it will over time improve their skills in creating accessible websites.

References

Brajnik, G. (2004) Comparing Accessibility Evaluation Tools: a method for tool effectiveness, *Universal Access in the Information Society*, **3** (3–4), 252–63.

Brajnik, G. (2005) Accessibility Assessments Through Heuristic Walkthroughs. In *Proceedings of HCItaly 2005, Simposio su Human–Computer Interaction, Rome, Italy, September 2005*, www.dimi.uniud.it/giorgio/publications.html#hcihw05.

Clark, J. (2003) *Building Accessible Websites*, Indianapolis, New Riders.

Coyne, K. and Nielsen, J. (2001) *Beyond ALT Text: making the web easy to use for users with disabilities*, Fremont, CA, Nielsen Norman Group.

Diaper, D. and Worman, L. (2003) Two Falls Out of Three in the Automated Accessibility Assessment of World Wide Websites: A-Prompt v. Bobby. In O'Neill, E., Johnson, P. and Palanque, P. (eds), *People and Computers XVII*, Berlin, Springer-Verlag, 349–64.

DRC (Disability Rights Commission) (2004) *The Web: access and inclusion for disabled people*, London, TSO, www.equalityhumanrights.com/en/publicationsandresources/Disability/Pages/Websiteaccessibilityguidance.aspx.

Eisma, R., Dickinson, A., Goodman, J., Syme, A., Tiwari, L. and Newell, A. (2004) Early User Involvement in the Development of Information Technology-related Products for Older People, *Universal Access in the Information Society*, **3** (2), 131-40.

Englefield, P., Paddison, C., Tibbits, B. and Damani, I. (2005) A Proposed Architecture for Integrating Accessibility Test Tools, *IBM Systems Journal*, **44** (3), 537-56.

Faulkner, S. and Arch, A. (2003) Accessibility Testing Software Compared. In *Proceedings of the Ninth Australian World Wide Web Conference (AusWeb '03), Gold Coast, Australia 5-9 July 2003*, http://ausweb.scu.edu.au/aw03/papers/arch/paper.html.

Georgia Tech Research Corporation (2004) *Accessibility in the User-centered Design Process*, www.ittatc.org/technical/access-ucd/contents.php.

Ivory, M. and Hearst, M. (2001) The State of the Art in Automating Usability Evaluation of User Interfaces, *ACM Computing Surveys*, **33** (4), 470-516.

Kelly, B., Phipps, L. and Swift, E. (2004) Developing a Holistic Approach for E-Learning Accessibility, *Canadian Journal of Learning and Technology*, **30** (3), www.ukoln.ac.uk/web-focus/papers/cjtl-2004.

Mankoff, J., Fait, H. and Tran, T. (2005) Is Your Web page Accessible? A comparative study of methods for assessing web page accessibility for the blind. In *Proceedings of ACM Conference on Human Factors in Computing Systems (CHI '05), Portland OR,* New York, ACM Press, 41-50.

Newell, A. and Gregor, P. (2000) User Sensitive Inclusive Design - in search of a new paradigm. In *Proceedings of First ACM Conference on Universal Usability (CUU 2000), Arlington VA, November 2000*, New York, ACM Press, 39-44.

Nielsen, J. (1994) Heuristic Evaluation. In Nielsen, J. and Mack, R. (eds) *Usability Inspection Methods*, New York, Wiley & Sons, 25-62.

Nielsen, J. (1999) *Alertbox: disabled accessibility - the pragmatic approach*, www.useit.com/alertbox/990613.html (accessed 22 December 2005).

Paddison, C. and Englefield, P. (2003) Applying Heuristics to Perform a Rigorous Accessibility Inspection in a Commercial Context, In *Proceedings of 2nd ACM Conference on Universal Usability (CUU 2003), Vancouver*, New York, ACM Press, 126-33.

Petrie, H., Hamilton, F., King, N. and Pavan, P. (2006) Remote Usability

Evaluations with Disabled People. In *Proceedings of ACM Conference on Human Factors in Computing Systems (CHI 2006), Montreal, Quebec,* New York, ACM Press.

Petrie, H., King, N. and Weisen, M. (2005) The Accessibility of Museum Websites: results from an English investigation and international comparisons. In Trant, J. and Bearman, D. (eds), *Museums and the Web 2005: Proceedings*, Toronto: Archives and Museum Informatics, www.archimuse.com/mw2005/papers/petrie/petrie.html.

Slatin, J. and Rush, S. (2002) *Maximum Accessibility: making the web more usable for everyone*, Boston, Pearson Education.

Sloan, D., Gregor, P., Booth, P. and Gibson, L. (2002) Auditing Accessibility of UK Higher Education Websites. In *Interacting with Computers*, **14** ,313-25.

Spindler, T. (2002) The Accessibility of Web Pages for Mid Sized College and University Libraries, *Reference and User Services Quarterly*, **42** (2), 149-54.

Thatcher, J. (2003) *Web Accessibility - what not to do*, www.jimthatcher.com/whatnot.htm.

Thatcher, J. (2006) Accessibility Testing. In Thatcher, J. et al., *Web Accessibility: web standards and regulatory compliance*, Friends of Ed.

Thompson, T., Burgstahler, S. and Comden, D. (2003) Research on Web Accessibility in Higher Education, *Information Technology and Disabilities*, **IX** (2), www.rit.edu/~easi/itd/itdv09n2/thompson.htm.

Vanderdonckt, J. and Beirekdar, A. (2005) Automated Web Evaluation by Guideline Review, *Journal of Web Engineering*, **4** (2), Rinton Press, 102-17.

W3C (2005) *Involving Users in Web Accessibility Evaluation*, World Wide Web Consortium (W3C), www.w3.org/WAI/eval/users.html (accessed 29 January 2006).

Waller, A., Balandin, S., O'Mara, D. and Judson, A. (2005) Training AAC Users in User-centred Design. In *Electronic Workshops in Computing Series - Proceedings of Accessible Design in the Digital World Conference, Dundee, Scotland 23-25 August 2005*, British Computer Society, www.bcs.org/server.php?show=ConWebDoc.3756.

URLs

1 http://validator.w3.org
2 http://jigsaw.w3.org/css-validator
3 http://validator.w3.org/checklink
4 www.visionaustralia.org.au/ais/toolbar

5 http://chrispederick.com/work/web-developer
6 http://lynx.browser.org
7 www.vischeck.com
8 www.visionaustralia.org.au/info.aspx?page=628
9 http://juicystudio.com/services/readability.php
10 www.usabilityexchange.com
11 www.wabcluster.org/uwem1

Chapter 7

Issues for library and information services

PETER BROPHY

Introduction

The practical implications of the need to ensure web accessibility are not always straightforward to assess. Few if any in the profession would argue against the aim of achieving as accessible a web presence as possible, but there is a variety of constraints which make achieving this objective difficult. Not least, libraries and information services have limited budgets and, much as staff may like to provide fully accessible services and equipment, the reality is that it is always a matter of choosing between conflicting demands. What is more, few libraries can afford to employ staff dedicated solely to accessibility and expert in its many ramifications: it is one requirement among many. Where, then, to start?

In this chapter it is suggested that a useful way forward is to adopt a sevenfold strategy:

1 Spend time listening to representatives of users and potential users, and couple this intelligence with sound professional judgement. If possible, conduct user testing of website features. Consider the users, the web-based services and the environments in which use will occur as a whole. In this way a picture can be built up of the library's specific user requirements, rather than the theoretical needs of every possible user group.
2 Become familiar with the key sources of advice and guidance, selectively concentrating on those which are most relevant to this user population.

3 Develop an accessibility policy for the library service that addresses the particular needs of its users.
4 Audit the existing web presence, including finding out which are the most visited pages and services (and thus the ones most in need of verification).
5 Introduce those changes which, the evidence suggests, will have maximum impact, and make the sometimes small adjustments that will benefit as many users as possible at minimum cost. (This will require judgement based on the mapping of the user requirements to guidelines and professional advice.)
6 Provide appropriate assistive technologies that meet the particular needs of the library's community.
7 Continually monitor and review what is being achieved, not least by continuing to listen to what the users, and the non-users, are saying.

It is worth stressing that accessibility is not just a matter of good website design, carried out in a vacuum, but arises at the interstice of the web page, the environment in which it is viewed and the user. As Kelly et al. (2005) put it, accessibility 'is experiential and environmental, it depends on the interaction of the content with the user agent, the assistive technology and the user'.

Listening to the user community

In an era when 'user-centred' services are accepted as the norm it may seem obvious that tackling the accessibility of web-based services should involve listening to the users, but it cannot be taken for granted that this always happens. A particular issue is that the problem of inaccessible internet services, including those delivered by other agencies, may have turned some users away from the library. Therefore the starting point must be engagement with users who have different accessibility requirements within the community at large, rather than simply among the existing active users of the service.

For many such potential users there will be representative groups and agencies that can be consulted. For example, in higher and further education institutions the Student Services Department will almost certainly have a brief to identify students with particular needs and to put in place appropriate strategies to ensure that they are not disadvantaged. In the commercial sector, human resource departments will be responsible for ensuring that employees are not discriminated against by reason of disability and will have access to specialist advice on how this can best be achieved. For public-facing services, such as those of the public library or the voluntary sector, things are not so straightforward. In such cases an active strategy of engagement with social services departments and with local voluntary agencies will be necessary. There may be an umbrella group (for an example see One Voice[1]) or it may be necessary to identify separate organizations.

Listening also involves seeking out opportunities to learn more about the factors that are preventing access to services, including the adequacy of solutions that have already been put in place. Inevitably this is something of a balancing act and it is all too easy to make the assumption that current, well-meaning actions have solved the problem. As I have remarked elsewhere in a somewhat different context, 'the library which claims to have resolved disability access problems because it has provided a ramp at the entrance has clearly not thought through the issue from the point of view of a blind person, whose access may even have been made more difficult!' (Brophy, 2005, 169). The same can all too easily happen with websites. And, as with the physical library, it is not just a matter of what is provided by the library, but also of how the intending user can get there.

Advice and guidelines

In determining what issues need to be considered, attention will be paid both to general approaches, such as Design for All (as described in Chapter 3), and to specific recommendations, including of course the W3C Web Accessibility Initiative (WAI) with its WCAG, ATAG and UAAG (see section on 'The Web Accessibility Initiative Guidelines' in Chapter 5). While the latter set of guidelines is very comprehensive, one of its problems is that it is difficult to interpret and prioritize for local situations, as well as being highly technical. Furthermore, too often accessibility is thought of as compliance to such guidelines; yet, as already indicated, it is far more than that, and must include consideration of both the people requiring access and their environment.

It is for this reason that interpretative guidelines have been developed by professionals in the library and information field, and these form a helpful source of more specific advice. A practical example is the checklist produced by IFLA, described as 'a practical tool for all types of libraries (public, academic, school, special) to 1) assess existing levels of accessibility to buildings, services, materials and programs and to 2) enhance accessibility where needed' (Irvall and Nielsen, 2005, 3). The checklist covers the whole range of library services, including physical access, but makes ten specific recommendations regarding web-based services, derived from WAI recommendations:

- make the design logical and easy to navigate
- make the children's web page accessible
- provide software to enlarge text, change font and contrast, length of lines, and space between lines
- give alternative formats to .pdf and .doc - preferably unformatted text (.txt)
- separate contents from design - use style sheets to guide presentation and layout
- include search capability on your website
- avoid frames and tables
- avoid moving figures and texts
- use relative measurements for text
- accompany audio with text. (Irvall and Nielsen, 2005, 15)

It should be noted that some of these recommendations differ significantly from WAI since they are intended as a simplified approach. For example, WAI does not prohibit the use of tables but mandates that they should contain markup to enable accessible browsers to transform them accurately, while IFLA suggests they should be avoided altogether (for examples of the issues and solutions see Starling Access Services[2]). Despite this reservation, the IFLA recommendations provide a good, practical starting point.

Another useful source of guidance can be found on the Australian Library and Information Association (ALIA) website.[3] These notes are focused on good web design, rather than specifically on accessibility, but they offer an excellent overview of issues and their overall approach is commendable - 'our overall design philosophy is one of simplicity'.

Accessibility policies

Advice is also available on the development of an accessibility policy for the library. As noted above, this policy needs to be specific to the local situation, not borrowed from somewhere else and slotted into place without much thought or amendment. The Office for Information Technology Policy (OITP) of the American Library Association (ALA) has published advice on accessibility policy development, based on work by the University of Washington's DO-IT initiative. The ALA suggests that 'a thoughtful and comprehensive accessibility policy demonstrates a library's commitment to meeting the needs of all patrons. A well drafted policy identifies how the library intends to accommodate the needs of patrons with disabilities and establish specific procedures for responding to requests in a timely manner' (ALA, 2007).

The following ten stages may be helpful in developing the policy:

1 As discussed above, listen to the community so as to establish its needs and any perceived barriers.
2 Analyse existing library policies, for example those which set out local web design standards, those which set out the library's requirements from its suppliers and those which deal with access by users to electronic resources.
3 Examine other organizations' policies in this area to see if they contain good ideas that could be adapted and adopted. Examples include:
   - Northampton College Accessibility Policy[4] - this also includes a report on actions taken.
   - Bedfordshire Virtual Library Accessibility Policy[5] - interesting because it is focused on a purely web-based service.
   - Oxford University Library Services Accessibility Statement[6] - a brief summary of web design principles adopted by the library.
4 Write an overarching statement of intent that sets out what the library is committing itself to. This needs to be realistic and achievable, and not simply a bland and meaningless aspiration.
5 List the specific action areas that will be addressed. For example, it may state that all web development will be standards based or that all text used on web pages will be resizable.
6 State who is responsible. It is good practice to have a manager identified as having overall responsibility in this area. However, this holds the danger that other staff will simply pass all accessibility-related issues over to that person. To avoid this, the policy should contain a statement on the responsibilities of all members of staff. The related area of staff training and development should also be addressed here.

7 State how information on accessibility will be disseminated.
8 Make a commitment to evaluate the accessibility of services on a regular basis, and say how this will be done.
9 Provide clear policy on how the library will open itself to comment and criticism and how it will respond.
10 Get endorsement of senior management and state this in the policy, along with the date it is agreed. Review and revise the policy at regular (perhaps annual) intervals.

Auditing accessibility

The assessment of website accessibility is covered elsewhere in this volume (Chapter 6, section on 'Conducting an accessibility audit'), so there is no need to go into detail here. What is worth stressing, however, is that it is imperative that accessibility is checked by human evaluators as well as by online tools. As Owen (2003) has pointed out, accessibility 'tools do not allow for the "human factor" of accessible design: they can tell you that an image is accessible because it has alternative text, but they cannot tell you whether the alternative text appropriately describes the image it is attached to'. More importantly, they do not relate accessibility to a specific user population and its particular needs. It is therefore important that part of the checking process involves finding out from users what they find difficult, as well as undertaking automated checks and using professional judgement.

UKOLN's QA Focus has published a number of case studies showing how libraries and library projects have addressed accessibility issues. They include:

- Edinburgh University Library Online,[7] which identified the problems in maintaining a website with in excess of 2000 pages. Key problems identified included:
  - 'The need to support older browsers
  - The sheer number of static pages
  - The amount of legacy code and use of tabular layouts.'
- The e-MapScholar project,[8] which was concerned with developing tools and learning and teaching materials to enhance and support the use of geospatial data. The development team noted that 'use of templates and CSS have helped in minimizing workload when a problem has been noted and the materials updated' and also commented

that 'user feedback from evaluations, user workshops and demonstrations has been extremely useful in identifying potential problems'.
- The Non-Visual Access to the Digital Library (NoVA) project,[9] which used a task-based approach with groups of sighted and visually impaired people to explore what the real barriers were. More information on this work will be found in Craven and Brophy (2003).

It is also worth looking carefully at some of the websites that have won awards for their accessibility. Among these are:

- Wakefield Libraries' *Speaking Volumes* website,[10] which won a 2006 Jodi Mates Award for Excellence
- *The History of Wolverhampton* from Wolverhampton Arts and Museums Service,[11] which was commended in the same awards
- the University of the West of England Library website,[12] which offers selectable contrast versions as well as a text-only option.

One of the reasons why libraries and information services need to monitor and review the accessibility of their services is that technological change constantly impacts on their service provision. For example, services based on Web 2.0 technologies, such as mashups, may or may not pose new accessibility problems for a library's users - they may also offer solutions. The only way to find out is to continue listening to, and observing, users in their real access contexts. Web 2.0 is discussed in greater detail below.

Actioning improved web design

Libraries do not always have total control over their web presence, often having to abide by corporate standards and sometimes having to make use of corporate or external web designers. It can thus be difficult to transform good intentions into practice. The identification of a manager with overall responsibility, suggested above, is part of the answer to this dilemma, but just as important is the establishment of an ongoing dialogue between the library, which defines the content of its web presence, and the designer.

It is often helpful to prioritize accessibility requirements. For example, some simple issues, such as good colour contrast and resizable text, may provide significant benefits and yet be easy to implement. Getting the designer, who will be able to estimate the effort involved, alongside in developing the priorities for action is therefore important.

To be effective, this process needs to be based on a checklist of accessibility features. WAI can be used, but a number of interpretations are available which both librarians and designers may find helpful. The IFLA approach was described above. Another example is the Royal National Institute of Blind People (RNIB) Web Access Centre, which provides 'Design and build checkpoints'.[13] These are grouped into:

- Cascading Style Sheets (CSS)
- colour
- images
- multimedia
- navigation
- text
- structure
- scripts and forms.

These recommendations are of course related to people who are blind or visually impaired and thus do not address all of the web accessibility issues, but they provide a very useful starting point. Indeed, if they are used alongside a Design for All philosophy then a very large proportion of the accessibility issues will be addressed.

More broadly, the development of database-driven websites, where the content and structure are separated, has significantly improved the potential for accessible services. The older model of static pages meant that HTML code was wrapped round the content and thus, in effect, inseparable from it. By placing the information content in a database and pulling it into the presentation when required, different structures can be applied to meet different users' needs.

Providing assistive technologies

There is a huge range of assistive technologies available to help people to make use of the web (see Chapter 2), but the problem for most libraries is that they have limited budgets, space and expertise to expend on this area. It is critical that the right choices are made so as to maximize the benefits of investment.

The first step must therefore be to discover exactly what technologies the users of any particular library need. Here the work already undertaken in listening to the users will be invaluable. Care needs to be taken, however, to ensure that the solutions adopted are usable and useful. An obvious example is that the latest version of a screenreader may be unfamiliar to many users and thus be less likely to be used than the version to which they are accustomed. The temptation, of course, is to get the most up-to-date version with all its additional features, but there is a balance to be struck. It is also important to configure the software and equipment appropriately. Jaws for Windows, for example, perhaps the most popular screenreader, can be configured to output to a variety of devices, including Braille displays. The question is, what will this library's users want?

The installation of assistive technologies needs to be undertaken with great care and sensitivity. It is poor practice, for example, to set aside one PC under a large notice that says, 'For the use of disabled users'. This is akin to attaching a label to the users themselves, pointing out that they are both disabled and different! The ideal would be for all PCs to have a comprehensive range of identical assistive technology so that a user with a disability could book or use a PC in the same way as anyone else. Where this cannot be achieved, specialist facilities should be provided in a discreet manner.

Once assistive technologies have been identified and installed, it is extremely important that staff are fully trained in their use - and this means part-time staff who may work in the evenings or at weekends as much as full-timers. Hannah (2003), for example, reported that at Gateshead 'screen magnification and speech synthesis software are available on all of our People's Network computers but staff training is required both in using the equipment and in assisting visually-impaired customers'. This last point is equally critical: will staff identify that a user is deaf, for example, and thus unable to use audio-based materials, without causing embarrassment? Will they know how to resolve a problem with the installed screenreader? Do they understand the accessibility features of standard packages such as Word or Excel?

Monitoring and reviewing accessibility

The achievement of accessible services will only be attained where the strategy is seen as requiring continuing effort. It is very easy to approach the task with enthusiasm, to address immediate problems, but then to allow other pressing issues to sideline the initial commitment. For this reason, there needs to be a policy commitment to continuous monitoring and review. There should also be some kind of accessibility performance indicator included in annual service review.

Most organizations do undertake some monitoring of their web-based services, if only to check whether pages are being used. This in itself can tell a story about accessibility, especially if special services have been introduced. However, because the needs of different users with disabilities are very different, it is probably only by asking and observing the actions of these users that a real insight will be gained. Two very simple ways to achieve this are to monitor the use of assistive technologies (if underused, why is this so? - was the wrong equipment installed perhaps?) and to maintain a careful watch on enquiries received. If library staff are continually being asked for help by a particular group of users, does this indicate that the service is inaccessible? (It may not, of course, but maintaining a watch on this type of demand often gives clues.)

Of the utmost importance is the practice of continuing to listen to the users. The seven-step process, introduced at the start of this chapter, is really an iterative one, as Figure 7.1 illustrates. What begins with listening carefully to the user community continues in the same way in a process of continual improvement.

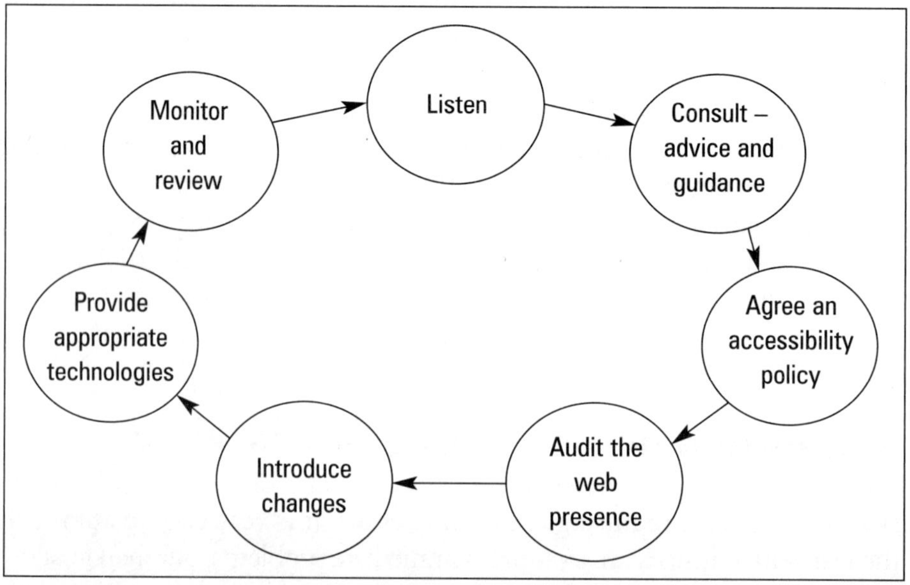

Figure 7.1 An iterative approach to ensuring accessibility

Other issues

Digitization and accessibility

Many libraries have been involved in digitization projects in recent years, but accessibility has not always been at the forefront of considerations. It is a great pity, and a considerable waste of resources, if a collection is digitized and only then is its accessibility addressed. Rather accessibility must be designed in from the start. The kinds of actions needed include:

- ensuring that video is captioned and audio described
- creating ALT text for all still images
- providing a transcript with audio recordings.

While the conversion of traditional print, audio and video resources into electronic formats has been a prominent part of libraries' activities in recent years, the creation of new electronic content (born-digital materials) is an issue of equal importance. Much of this latter content is complex and may be related to cultural or learning applications rather than straight information sources. There is much to be learned from other communities in this regard. As an example, the JISC TechDis service has recently suggested the use of an Accessibility Passport. Noting, and in so doing reflecting the earlier discussion in this chapter, that 'whether a learning object is accessible to the user depends on many factors: the abilities of the learner, the disposition of the lecturer, the policies of the institution as well as the time, place and medium of delivery', TechDis argues that it would be beneficial to record accessibility features alongside the individual objects. This work is linked to that of the Centre for Educational Technology and Interoperability Standards (CETIS) and of the IMS specification, which is responsible for e-learning technology standards. IMS has suggested that there are six principles which should be followed in making e-learning, or 'online distributed learning' as it terms it, accessible:

1. Allow for customization based on user preference.
2. Provide equivalent access to auditory and visual content based on user preference.
3. Provide compatibility with assistive technologies and include complete keyboard access.
4. Provide context and orientation information.

5 Follow IMS specifications and other relevant specifications, standards and/or guidelines.
6 Consider the use of XML.[14]

While the last of these may seem out of place, in fact XML opens up the possibility of Web 2.0 (and thus Library 2.0) type applications where the meaning of content can be interpreted by software. It is thus of very great importance for future accessibility initiatives.

Third-party content

Libraries usually have to deal with content supplied by third parties and are therefore dependent on the format which has been used for publication. While some web-based material may need to be redigitized to provide access, it is fairly obvious that most libraries will not have the capacity to undertake this except on rare occasions. Equally, it would be extremely wasteful for each library in the country to deal separately with such material.

There are a number of practical steps that can be taken to deal with this situation. First, where web-based material is found to be inaccessible for no good reason, for example because of poor attention to accessibility by the publisher, libraries should not hesitate in bringing this to the third party's attention. The more this is done, the more likely that future versions will comply! Second, care needs to be taken when a new service is brought into use to make sure that the right browser plug-ins (and the right versions of those plug-ins) are installed. Third, as ever, the performance of the new service needs to be monitored.

Another approach, where materials are found to be inaccessible, is to share the load, initially by contacting national services or other libraries that may have had to deal with the same material. An obvious source is Revealweb,[15] although most of its records relate to alternatives to traditional formats rather than to electronic documents.

Procurement

Linked to the above issue of third-party content is the whole question of procurement and the way in which accessibility is built into negotiations and contractual arrangements. Again, this may be an area where the library needs to work with its own institution to ensure that the necessary terms and conditions are applied. With library-specific systems it is important that accessibility features are specified at an early stage, preferably in the invitation to tender or equivalent. It may be noted that accessibility is included in the United Kingdom Core Specification (UKCS),[16] which contains over 500 requirements covering bibliographic database management, OPAC and end-user services, circulation control, acquisitions, serials control, document delivery, interlibrary loans and management information.

In both procurement and the use of third-party content librarians need to make their voices heard when barriers to accessibility are detected. Whether this is through their institutions and local authorities or through professional groups, there is an onus on professionals to be the champions of the excluded. If commercial, or indeed public sector, organizations are selling products into the library and information service market which are denying access to any group of users, they need to be challenged and, if they do not respond, the issue should be publicly exposed. Certainly, accessibility should be a mandatory requirement for all services and systems which a library purchases.

Looking to the future: Web 2.0

Web 2.0 developments hold out the prospect of making real inroads into the vast quantity of inaccessible content on the web. In essence, the meaning and characteristics of content will be described in a way that is processable by computers - so, for example, the detailed conformance of a web page to the WAI Guidelines will be capable of automatic querying. Users could then instruct their browsers only to deliver content that conformed with a particular guideline. Some interesting examples of this kind of product are starting to emerge. For example, Segala's *Search Thresher* extension for Firefox[17] tags Google search results with a red cross if they are not conformant according to their content labels, or a green tick if they are. To date, little content is labelled in this way, but the system demonstrates the potential for much more 'intelligent' services.

However, there are also dangers in this approach, and particularly in the development of more dynamic web pages where data is processed within the page and content is dynamically refreshed. Sliwa (2006, 12) has pointed out that

> a Web 2.0 application might make use of Asynchronous JavaScript and XML (AJAX) and Dynamic HTML to update information in a table without having to refresh an entire web page. But screen readers, magnifiers and other assistive technology may not know which parts of the page have changed unless developers take steps to make sure the tools can glean that information.

In effect, an accessible web page could suddenly and without warning become inaccessible - even as it is being viewed!

Conclusions

Accessibility is a very large subject, especially in networked environments where the opportunities to provide individual one-to-one assistance are limited. If web content is not immediately accessible to a user, it is probably not accessible at all. For this reason, and not simply because of legislative requirements, all libraries and information services need to be systematic in doing what they can to ensure that their services are truly inclusive.

At the same time, the realities of service provision are that the resources available are always limited, with the inevitable result that it is simply not possible to do everything that could be done - no library can employ an army of accessibility experts ready to double-check every web page and service that is offered. Furthermore, because libraries rely so much on external information they do not have the detailed control over the product that many manufacturers or other types of service may have.

Despite these constraints, a careful, planned approach to accessibility can produce excellent results. Perhaps the most critical determinant of success is the extent to which library staff listen to users and observe their needs. No single set of guidelines can address the needs of all library users and would-be users, because every community is different. Hence a clear understanding of what is likely to prove a barrier to the library's own local user group is critical.

There are many useful guidelines to draw on, a selection of which have been outlined in this chapter. Some are dealt with in greater detail in other chapters in this volume. Again, selectivity is the key: selectivity in relation to disability, and selectivity in relation to the expertise and resources available. A clear policy and plan is needed to guide library staff and any others involved in service development, such as web designers. A continual process of auditing the web presence and monitoring its accessibility is needed, with a judicious approach to making changes where they are necessary. Assistive technologies need to be appropriate to the user community.

Finally, library and information service staff need to keep a eye on current and future developments. As Web 2.0 services become available, are they opening up new possibilities for users with disabilities, or closing down services? Even where the staff do not have control they can exert influence, by making their voices heard on behalf of those who are in danger of exclusion. That is a professional responsibility which must be taken very seriously indeed.

References

American Library Association (2007) *Creating a Library Accessibility Policy*, www.ala.org/ala/washoff/oitp/emailtutorials/accessibilitya/22.cfm.

Brophy, P. (2005) *The Academic Library*, Facet Publishing.

Craven, J. and Brophy, P. (2003) *Non-visual Access to the Digital Library: the use of digital library interfaces by blind and visually impaired people* (Library and Information Commission Report 145), Centre for Research in Library and Information Management, www.cerlim.ac.uk/projects/nova.html.

Hannah, K. (2003) Developing Accessible Library Services, *CILIP Update,* **2** (11), 50-2.

Irvall, B. and Nielsen, G. S. (2005) *Access to Libraries for Persons with Disabilities: checklist* (IFLA Professional Reports 89), International Federation of Library Associations and Institutions.

Kelly, B. et al. (2005) Forcing Standardization or Accommodating Diversity? A framework for applying the WCAG in the real world, *Proceedings of the 2005 International Cross-Disciplinary Workshop on Web Accessibility (W4A)*, www.ukoln.ac.uk/web-focus/papers/w4a-2005/.

Owen, J. (2003) Making Your Website Accessible, *CILIP Update*, **2** (1), 48-9.

Sliwa, C. (2006) Accessibility Issue Comes to a Head, *CompterWorld*, **40** (19) http://computerworld.com/action/article.do?command=viewArticleBasic&articleId=111219.

URLs

1 www.onevoicedisabilityservices.org

2 www.starlingweb.com/acc/actab.htm

3 www.alia.org.au/alianet/technical.notes.html

4 www.northamptoncollege.ac.uk/library/accessibility.pdf
5 www.galaxy.bedfordshire.gov.uk/webingres/bedfordshire/vlib/0.beds_libraries/about_this_site.htm#Accessibility
6 www.ouls.ox.ac.uk/accessibility
7 www.ukoln.ac.uk/qa-focus/documents/case-studies/case-study-26
8 www.ukoln.ac.uk/qa-focus/documents/case-studies/case-study-04
9 www.ukoln.ac.uk/qa-focus/documents/case-studies/case-study-11
10 www.speakingvolumesonline.org.uk
11 www.wolverhamptonhistory.org.uk
12 www.uwe.ac.uk/library
13 www.rnib.org.uk/xpedio/groups/public/documents/PublicWebsite/public_checkpoints.hcsp
14 www.imsglobal.org/accessibility/accessiblevers/sec3.html
15 www.revealweb.org.uk
16 www.cilip.org.uk/informationadvice/infomanagement/collection/corespecification.htm
17 http://segala.com/products/search-thresher

Chapter 8

Design for All in the library and information science curriculum

RICHARD ESKINS, JENNY CRAVEN

Introduction

The importance of providing appropriate training and awareness on the topic of web accessibility cannot be stressed enough, for without a proper understanding of accessibility issues and of the tools and techniques to apply accessible design to websites and web applications, the widening of access for as many people as possible will be severely hampered.

Before even considering training in the design of accessible websites, a more fundamental approach to the issues is needed. General disability awareness training will provide a wider understanding of how different impairments can affect people, and thus enable more informed decisions to be made on the provision of accessible resources and on how to work with people who may have different access requirements. For example, when considering the requirements of blind and visually impaired people it is useful to understand the different types of impairments that can be experienced (only a small percentage of people who are 'blind' have no sight at all), so in some cases it may be necessary to provide screenreading assistive technologies or scanners, but in others simply providing large monitors can greatly improve accessibility for a considerable number of people with visual impairments.

At the very least, an understanding of how different assistive technologies work with operating systems and with websites is important. However, training in the use of the assistive technologies provided is equally important, so that, in the case of a library, staff can help visitors to use the software provided on the open access PCs.

Many organizations offer such training. For example, the RNIB offers a range of training courses, both in-house and public, aimed at designers, developers and content authors as well as website owners, project managers and marketing personnel,[1] and the Force Foundation charity[2] has been working with librarians in developing countries to help make their libraries (and websites) more accessible (primarily for print-impaired people) and has run workshops on this topic in Latin and Central America and in Vietnam (Owen, Craven and Maskort, 2007).

Design for All

The design of accessible websites is often referred to as 'Design for All'. This term can be a little overwhelming at times because 'except for a very limited range of products, "design for all" is very difficult' (Newell and Gregor, 2001), not least because the provision of access for people with a particular access requirement can often make access difficult for someone with a different requirement. However, it is generally accepted that the concept of Design for All (DfA) shows a commitment to designing, developing and commissioning/procuring products and services (such as websites) which can reach as wide an audience as possible (see also Chapter 3, section on 'What is "Design for All"').

'Design for All' in a library environment means that library information technology (IT) systems and interfaces must be designed in a way that enables them to be read and interacted with easily by all users of the library, whether they are physically visiting the library or are accessing it remotely, and regardless of any disability or access preference they may have. The Royal National Institute for Blind People (RNIB) describes 'design for all' in relation to websites as 'a single version of the website which is accessible to everyone' and states that 'well designed graphics and multimedia are a positive aid to using and understanding websites, and do not need to be sacrificed for accessibility' (RNIB, 2005). This is a general shift away from the provision of parallel 'accessible' websites, such as the provision of a text-only version, to the provision of a single version that is fully accessible.

The UK Cabinet Office report on the accessibility of government online services across the EU makes a recommendation to the software industry that all web designers must be trained in DfA accessibility requirements and techniques. The Cabinet Office recommendations should be taken further, to ensure all courses and modules relating to web design have accessibility built into them, rather than being offered as an add-on. The library and information sector should be no exception.

This issue was explored in a survey of textbooks on web design, which revealed that accessibility is generally treated as an add-on rather than as a fundamental part of the design process, and thus students learning web design view accessibility features as 'something you go back and throw in at the end, after you've done the important stuff' (Rosmaita, 2006). Using these findings as a basis, an approach has been developed to address the issue. The 'Accessibility First' approach makes accessibility the focus of the course so that 'all aspects of web design should be taught from the standpoint of how they contribute to accessibility' (Rosmaita, 2006). Furthermore, if this approach is adopted from the start of the course, students will consider it the natural way to approach web design.

DfA is the focus of an Information Society Technologies (IST) Coordination Action: 'Design for All for eInclusion', the objectives of which include:

- Extend the uptake of DfA within the ICT Industry in Europe (Objective 5).
- Establish suitable criteria, structures and content for the creation of both online and offline courses for Design for All for eInclusion for a wide range of stakeholders, e.g. designers, business executives, user groups, undergraduates (modules) and postgraduates (MSc degree level) (Objective 6).[3]

DfA in the curriculum has also been addressed by the Design for All Network of Excellence (D4ALLnet) (EU Information Society Technologies Programme) set up in 2001. D4ALLnet aims to set up networks of excellence in DfA across Europe to 'integrate information and identify core knowledge sets and skills for model curricula in design for all specifically for information and communication products, systems and services' (Nicolle, Rundle and Graupp, 2001). The knowledge and skills sets proposed by D4ALLnet include:

- Design for All awareness: to encourage students to think about the diverse needs of users and how barriers may be put up when understanding of user needs is not fully understood. (See also Chapter 2)
- Ethical, legal and commercial considerations: including inclusive solutions and equal opportunities to DfA; legislative frameworks; commercial benefits of DfA. (See also Chapter 4)
- Recommendations: awareness of the principles, guidelines, standards and recommendations available. (See also Chapters 5 and 6)
- Interpersonal skills for teamwork: providing students with the necessary skills to convince co-workers of the importance of DfA and the solutions provided.
- Accessible content: teaching students about current methods and techniques to produce accessible content, or to convert content to become more accessible.
- Accessible interaction: teaching students about different assistive technologies and adaptive devices which help enable accessibility. (See also Chapter 3)
- New paradigms of interaction: looking to new and emerging issues. (For example, issues described in Chapter 10)
- User centred design: teach students about the philosophies and methodologies relating to users and usability/accessibility issues.

(Velasco et al., 2004).

Web accessibility training resources

For information professionals there is a variety of training opportunities available through commercial trainers, ad hoc courses and online resources.

Sue Hill Recruitment[4] is an employment agency for the UK library and information sector. Its view is that web development skills and an understanding of accessibility and usability are essential, not least because these skills are appearing in many job descriptions, but also because 'if websites are to be the windows into organizations of the future someone needs to know how to do it properly' and 'because website skills are transferable to intranet skills [and] intranets are all about content and knowledge management' (quote from Sue Hill). Although this is seen from a UK perspective, the situation is likely to be similar in other countries such as the USA where a quick look at the American Library Association's JobList[5] brings up posts such as Web Librarian and Media and Digital

Services Librarian, both requiring web development skills along with a professional degree in Library and Information Science.

Before looking for a trainer it could be helpful to read the Web Accessibility Initiative (WAI) document entitled 'Curricula for web accessibility training'[6]. This provides some idea of the sort of curriculum that should be included in an accessibility training course. The following sections of this chapter will now look at training opportunities in some depth.

Commercial trainers

The name Jakob Nielsen is synonymous with web usability and accessibility. The Nielsen Norman Group[7] offers a series of training opportunities at different locations around the world. Although the focus is on usability, including web usability, intranet usability and content usability, it should be recognized that usability is a fundamental aspect of ensuring any website or intranet is accessible. The Nielsen Norman Group also publishes reports (for example, see Coyne and Nielsen, 2001) and Jakob Nielsen produces his own bi-weekly column called Alertbox[8] which discusses a variety of usability and accessibility issues.

Other commercial trainers include Open Interface[9] in Dublin, which runs Accessible Design for Webmasters; London-based usability consultants Userfocus[10] offer web accessibility for developers/designers; consultancy, training and research specialists System Concepts offer accessibility and usability training and events; and the Ark Group[11] works globally with a portfolio of events, including sessions on web usability (which includes the issue of accessibility). There are also many commercial trainers, such as GBDirect, who offer web accessibility training as part of their comprehensive training portfolio.

Netskills[13] was originally a project funded by the Joint Information Systems Committee (JISC) Electronic Libraries (e-Lib) programme. Based at the University of Newcastle, Netskills is now a service that provides training and training materials to UK higher and further education institutions and the public sector. Issues relating to web accessibility are central to many Netskills workshops and training material modules, from the need for valid, semantically structured HTML to the advantages of Cascading Style Sheets and considerations when working with software such as DreamWeaver or Flash.

More specifically, Netskills' one-day workshop 'Accessibility, Usability and Your Web Site'[14] provides a more holistic approach to web accessibility, posing that an understanding of the different ways in which people interact with the web is the key to providing a better online experience for everyone, regardless of ability. The workshop provides a thorough and up-to-date overview of current legislation and guidelines, from the Disability Discrimination Act (DDA) to Disability Equality Duty (DED) and Web Content Accessibility Guidelines (WCAG) 1.0 to WCAG 2.0. Real-world issues are also highlighted and the need for user-focused web design is introduced. Netskills also provides a web accessibility and usability testing service and has carried out evaluations and audits for both research and information focused websites within the HE and FE communities.

Online resources

There are a number of examples of online training resources. The Web Accessibility Evaluation Curriculum[15] describes its curriculum as 'a unified training resource for Web Accessibility evaluators who want to do evaluation of websites against an evaluation methodology that has been harmonized at a European level and in the context of Web Accessibility certification'. This provides an excellent overview of web accessibility issues in Europe, followed by a very informative section on how people with disabilities use the web. It also provides detail on the Web Content Accessibility Guidelines[16] and how they can be used in website evaluation.

The Barrier Free Web Design postgraduate course[17] has been developed at Johannes Kepler University in Linz, Austria. It offers a comprehensive university course on accessible web design that is delivered mainly online and is designed in an accessible way for both students and teachers (Miesenberger and Ortner, 2006). The Barrier Free Web Design course follows similar topics to those identified by Velasco et al. (2004), including:

- technical fundamentals
- assistive technologies
- guidelines and laws
- accessibility
- design and usability
- practical experience.

(Miesenberger and Ortner, 2006, 254)

While not a training resource, TechDis[18] provides a wealth of advice and tools on barrier-free design of resources. These include the Web Accessibility Self-Evaluation Tool, 'A Dyslexic Perspective On E-Content Accessibility' and advice on assistive technologies. There is also a series of guides called TechDis Accessibility Essentials. These explain how to make electronic documents more readable, how to write accessible documents in MS Word and how to make presentations accessible. Although directed at the UK further and higher education sectors, this site provides information that can help the information professional.

Likewise, the UK Royal National Institute of Blind People's (RNIB) Web Access Centre[19] provides a wealth of resources. This includes two open training sessions entitled 'Demystifying accessibility' and 'Accessibility – beyond the basics'. It also provides bespoke in-house training covering all aspects of web accessibility. The Web Access Centre provides consultancy services such as website accessibility audits and advice for those implementing accessibility features to a new or redesigned site. It gives an overview of accessibility standards such as the WCAG and its own See It Right guidelines.[20] The See It Right guidelines build on the Web Accessibility Initiative Guidelines to provide a series of checkpoints that are particularly focused on accessibility for users with sight problems.

Flow Interactive Limited[21] supplies accessibility audits, being a See It Right certified company. Its training courses include web usability and user-centred design. Webcredible[22] provides a wide range of technical solutions for accessible web design and runs courses on both web usability and web accessibility.

Ad hoc training

Various training courses are often offered by university departments or as part of conference packages. For example, the Department of Information Studies at Sheffield runs day courses on accessibility awareness, mostly aimed at the higher education and commercial sectors. Middlesex University has run a summer school on Design for All in ICT, which includes looking at assistive technologies, checking and evaluating web accessibility and learning about standards and legislation. Charities such as AbilityNet[23] offer training in the use of assistive technologies that can give a greater insight into the needs of the disabled user, and the Shaw Trust offers an Essential Web Accessibility Workshop.[24]

Conferences such as UMBRELLA,[25] (which is the biennial meeting organized in the UK by the Chartered Institute of Library and Information Professionals (CILIP)), Internet World (REF) and the World Library and Information Conference (WILIC),[26] have themes and discussions on accessibility of electronic resources.

Web accessibility in the job market

Scan over current job adverts for information professionals and you will soon notice that web page or web content development has become an integral part of many professional posts. ICT skills, although still featuring in many adverts, have long been an accepted essential and now we see adverts that contain descriptions such as 'you will be responsible for the library web pages', '[you will] take editorial responsibility for a web area' or '[you will] maintain the content of our intranet pages' and even roles requiring 'experience of Web 2.0 technologies'.

The starting place for many information professionals is at university, studying Library and Information Science in a variety of flavours or guises at undergraduate or postgraduate level. Traditionally, graduates have gone into a variety of roles, such as children's librarian, information officer, cataloguer, information broker and also diverse professions such as IT and the law!

Like a generation of graduates before, where many IT-literate graduates 'slipped' into library systems roles, many since 1994/5 have 'slipped' into web-related roles as a growing amount of resources have become web based. As illustrated above, many posts now have an integral web element at a variety of levels. These are not web developer posts, but information professional posts that use the web as 'another' information delivery tool, whether an intranet, a portal or a section of a larger site. The very focus of the adverts means that web developer is not the overriding skill required. What is required is an information professional with those expected ICT skills, which now include a level of web development knowledge and understanding.

So are current graduates joining the job market with the web development box ticked? More importantly, are they further equipped to understand beyond the basics of coding web pages and are they able to address the issues of web accessibility?

Teaching library and information students at Manchester Metropolitan University (MMU), lecturers at the Department of Information and Communications have seen changes over the last ten years in relation to the growth of the internet, web-based resource provision and the development of web-related courses and course modules. The approach taken to web accessibility (and usability) has been to plough a straight line in keeping things simple, ensuring that the focus has remained on the user and the information. Keeping a close watch on the design-led boom and bust of dot.com has led to the slow realization that usable (and accessible) is perhaps best. The legal world has also caught up with this through legislation such as Section 508 in the USA, the Disability Discrimination Act 1995 and the Special Educational Needs and Disability Act 2001 (see also Chapter 4, section 'Legal and policy factors').

However, the situation is changing once again, as the Web 2.0 revolution is under way, allowing the development of a variety of interactive browser-based applications. Once again it seems that accessibility is taking a back seat as these new and exciting applications are developed that often require people to have the skills, dexterity and sheer willingness to interact with the correct buttons and boxes (see also Chapter 10).

Figure 8.1 illustrates trends in web design, showing how the usable/accessible web ploughs a straight and steady line, while fashions such as the design-led sites of the dot.com boom and now Web 2.0 often leave usability/accessibility behind in the search for new and exciting interfaces and widgets to entertain and attract.

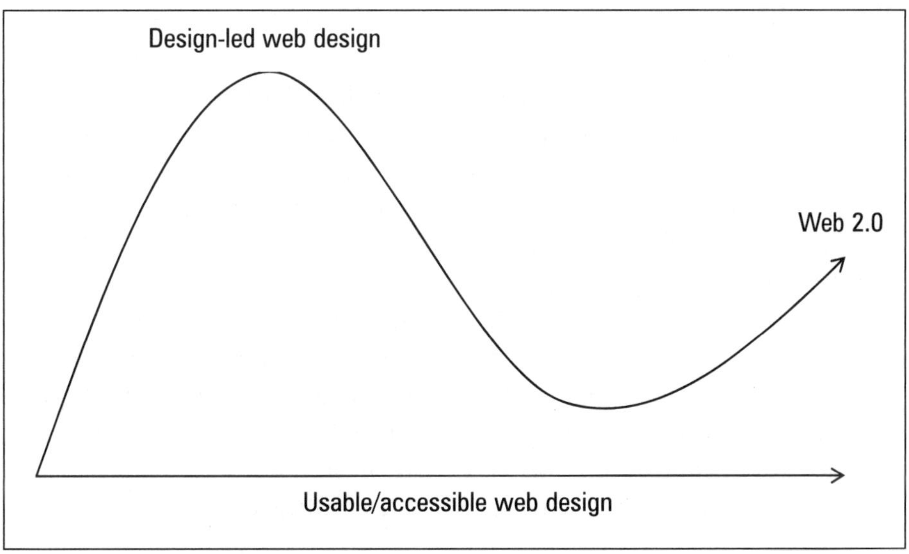

Figure 8.1 Trends in web design

Examples of web accessibility in the LIS curricula

At Manchester Metropolitan University (MMU) Department of Information and Communications[27] basic web design, which includes an introduction to accessibility, is core at both undergraduate and postgraduate levels. At undergraduate level web design can be taken as an elective in years two and three. This advances the practical skills beyond Notepad and simple XHTML, but always has an underlying theme of usability and accessibility. With a mixture of students of varying abilities, some more technical than others, some may have an eye for design, some may have the skills to produce and edit content. The type and quality of work can vary greatly, but if the student has followed the brief and adhered to standards and guidelines they can still be successful.

Accessibility is built into all assessments, which include the use of Web Accessibility Initiative Guidelines, use of validated code, use of Cascading Style Sheets to separate content from structure, and implementation of tools such as style switchers, skip navigation links etc. Issues such as colour contrast, accessible tables and informative title attributes are also embedded into the ethos of the module.

MMU makes full use of a university-wide licence for Netskills training materials. These materials include workbooks and lecture slides developed by Netskills at Newcastle University, which can be amended locally by the tutor to fit their needs (within the terms of the licence and copyright agreement). Besides the practical elements of XHTML and CSS they include workbooks on topics such as accessible web design, accessible web page content, and accessibility tips and tools. The combination of practical web design using standards and the theories of good usability is used to ensure that students see beyond their own little developments and think about the user experience - something that it seems has always been a core part of traditional LIS training.

The picture on many UK Library and Information Science (LIS) related courses is very similar. The Department of Information Studies in Sheffield[28] runs a module called Designing Usable Websites. Aimed at both postgraduate and undergraduate students, this introduces themes of usability and accessibility in terms of online information delivery. It includes an introduction called 'What is usability and why we care' and a further session on accessibility.

Up until October 2007, the Department of Information Studies at the University of Wales Aberystwyth[29] ran a module on electronic publishing. The module started by looking at quality criteria and evaluation of websites, before moving into the role of the 'webmaster', information architecture, design and the creation of a small website. Web accessibility issues were included in the introduction to the module, including the use of ALT text, clear design, colour contrast and text-only links. A small percentage of marks for the final project was given for adherence to good practice in this area.

The Graduate School of Informatics at the University of Strathclyde[30] began teaching web design as part of the IT core of the MSc Information and Library Studies in semester one from October 2007. This consists of sessions in hand coding and sessions using DreamWeaver, and includes materials on web accessibility.

The Department of Information Science at Loughborough University[31] teaches web design and authoring to undergraduates and design and authoring to postgraduates. The basis for both modules is the teaching of web standards and use is made of Notepad in order to get the students to understand code (for the importance of this, see also Chapter 5). This encourages students to create pages that are inherently accessible. The assessed work for both modules involves students designing and creating their own web pages - part of the criteria of assessment is the extent to which the pages are accessible to a wide audience.

The Information and Communication Studies Department at the University of Northumbria[32] teaches three different web-related modules. The first is entitled 'Presentation and Layout Technologies' (P&LT) and introduces students to creating valid markup using XHTML and internal stylesheets. The second is called 'Web Page Development' and leads on from P&LT. This focuses on the provision, design and maintenance of accessible and usable websites using XHTML and CSS for a range of clients. It goes on to cover XML, Document Type Definitions (DTDs) and XML-related technologies. The final module is at postgraduate level and is called 'Hypermedia for the Information Professional' - again this distinguishes what accessible and usable websites are and familiarizes students with some of the principles of effective website design.

The School of Library, Archive and Information Studies at University College London[33] teaches web publishing, which covers accessibility and usability and its legal, social and practical aspects. Standards are taught as part of wider course called 'How to make a website'.[34] The focus is on enabling LIS professionals to go into their professional setting knowing enough about the standards and technology to liaise with the web team, if not manage a website themselves. In eight weeks, students go from scratch to XHTML with CSS, covering the W3C and the Web Accessibility Guidelines along the way. While postgraduates may not go on to be web designers themselves, it is important that they know enough about the framework - guidelines, where to find standards, and how to meet the legal and social standards - so that when they go into a professional setting they can inform and ensure that the web designers adhere to those regulations and standards.

Other course examples include the Department of Archive and Library Sciences at the Ionian University in Greece.[35] Web design is taught here as part of the multimedia course. Though advanced web design programs such as DreamWeaver provide accessibility support, the students are taught to apply accessibility principles through code elements using XHTML and CSS, as structural and presentational elements respectively. Throughout the course, students are encouraged to apply, as a minimum, fundamental accessibility recommendations such as the application of ALT text tags and ID elements. They are also encouraged to test their web pages for compliance with a number of different web browsers.

Conclusions

Training and awareness in web accessibility and Design for All is vital to ensure knowledge and key skills are acquired by those who will be responsible for procuring, providing, designing and developing accessible resources and services such as websites. Many organizations and institutions are already addressing this by providing training courses and online tutorials and including accessibility and Design for All in the curriculum to ensure all courses and modules relating to web design have accessibility built into them, rather than as an add-on. Drawing on the work of Velasco et al. (2004) and Miesenberger and Ortner (2006), key areas which should be considered by organizations and institutes for their training programmes and course and curriculum development should include:

- Design for All awareness
- ethical, legal and commercial considerations

- guidelines, principles, standards and recommendations available
- accessibility methods and techniques to produce accessible content, or to convert content to be more accessible
- assistive technologies and adaptive devices
- design and usability, including user-centred design methodologies
- practical experience, including skills to promote accessibility in the work environment.

References

Coyne, P. and Nielsen, J. (2001) *Beyond ALT Text: making the web easy to use for users with disabilities and how to conduct usability evaluations for accessibility*, Freemont, Nielsen Norman Group.

Miesenberger, K. and Ortner, D. (2006) Raising the Expertise of Web Designers Through Training: the experience of BFWD - accessible web design (Barrierefreies Webdesign) in Austria. In Miesenberger, K. et al. (eds), *Computers Helping People with Special Needs: 10th international conference, ICCHP Linz, July 2006 proceedings*, New York, Springer, 253-7.

Newell, A. F. and Gregor, P. (2001) User Sensitive Inclusive Design, *JIM 2001 Interaction Homme/Machine and Assistance, 4-6 July 2001*, 18-20.

Nicolle, C., Rundle, C. and Graupp, H. (2001) Towards Curricula in Design for All for Information and Communication Products, Systems and Services. In *Proceedings of INCLUDE 2003, 23-26 March, London.*

Owen, D., Craven, J. and Maskort, J. (2007) The Force Foundation: opening up a work of print, *New Beacon*, **14**, February, 34-7.

Rosmaita, B. J. (2006) Accessibility First! A new approach to web design, *SIGCSE '06 March 1-5 2006, Houston, Texas, USA.*

Royal National Institute of Blind People (RNIB) (2005) Background on Web Accessibility, www.rnib.org.uk/xpedio/groups/public/documents/publicWebsite/public_Webaccessibility.hcsp.

Velasco, C. A. et al. (2004) IDCnet: inclusive design curriculum network - first results. In Miesenberger, K. et al. (eds), *Computers Helping People with Special Needs: 9th International Conference, ICCHP Paris, July 2004 proceedings*, New York, Springer, 110-16.

URLs

1 www.rnib.org.uk/xpedio/groups/public/documents/PublicWebsite/public_webacctraining.hcsp

2 www.f-force.nl
3 www.dfaei.org/objectives.html
4 www.suehill.com
5 http://joblist.ala.org
6 www.w3.org/WAI/training/cr
7 www.nngroup.com
8 www.useit.com/alertbox
9 www.openinterface.ie
10 www.userfocus.co.uk
11 www.ark-group.com
12 http://ebusiness.gbdirect.co.uk
13 www.netskills.ac.uk/content/index.html
14 www.netskills.ac.uk/content/products/onsite/range/access.html
15 www.support-eam.org/waec/en/index.html
16 www.w3.org/WAI/intro/wcag.php
17 www.bfwd.at
18 www.techdis.ac.uk 8
19 www.rnib.org.uk/xpedio/groups/public/documents/code/public_rnib008789.hcsp
20 www.rnib.org.uk/xpedio/groups/public/documents/PublicWebsite/public_wai.hcsp#P8_632
21 www.flow-interactive.com
22 www.webcredible.co.uk
23 www.abilitynet.org.uk
24 www.shaw-trust.org.uk/page/3/59/312
25 www.umbrella2007.org.uk
26 www.ifla.org/IV/ifla72/index.htm
27 www.hlss.mmu.ac.uk/infocomms
28 www.shef.ac.uk/is
29 www.dil.aber.ac.uk/en/home.asp
30 www.cis.strath.ac.uk
31 http://info.lut.ac.uk/departments/dils
32 http://northumbria.ac.uk/sd/academic/ceis
33 www.ucl.ac.uk/slais
34 www.ucl.ac.uk/slais/melissa-terras/webpublishing
35 www.ionio.gr/central/en/university

Chapter 9

Best practice examples of web accessibility

JENNY CRAVEN

Introduction

This chapter provides some examples of what is often referred to as 'best practice', the aim being to illustrate some of the areas relating to web accessibility covered elsewhere in this book with examples of good practice. The term 'best practice' can be defined as 'a technique, method, process, activity, incentive or reward that is more effective at delivering a particular outcome than any other technique, method, process, etc.' (Wikipedia, 2007). The term is also discussed in relation to developing approaches to finding and implementing best practice, where best practice is defined as 'the best way of doing things in the sector (or [outside] the sector if useful examples can be found)' (Brophy, 2006, 149).

The term should be treated with a little caution, however, as it can be open to interpretation and will depend on who is making the judgement that something is deemed to be 'best practice'. For the purposes of this chapter, best practice will simply refer to examples of good working practices, initiatives and projects relating to web accessibility. It is not an exhaustive list, as evidence of best practice can sometimes be difficult to identify in literature or in library promotional material, perhaps because libraries are simply getting on with the job of providing an accessible and interesting website that will meet the needs of as many of their visitors as possible, but may not be actively promoting or reporting on it. Therefore, the examples provided here intend to demonstrate how web accessibility is being addressed through evidence of improving access to resources and to the overall experience; raising awareness of accessibility issues; studies undertaken to explore specific issues relating to web accessibility; and finally, activities and/or initiatives undertaken to improve and encourage access for all - including the importance of involving users in the process.

Enhancing the overall web experience

There is evidence of good work being undertaken not only to improve access to web resources, but also to enhance the overall experience. For example, Walsh (2006) describes some innovative ways in which visual content has been made accessible to visually impaired people. Examples include an online art exhibition presenting six works of art. Each work has a link to an audio description (which is presented as a speaker icon with alternative text). Descriptions break down each feature of a painting (colour, concepts, background etc.) and also provide an interactive feedback feature so that visitors can submit evaluations of their experience. While this simple addition to the online experience has been designed with visually impaired people in mind, it could be attractive to a variety of other visitors who wished to combine the visual experience with an auditory experience. Another example (Walsh, 2006) is of the Flash Map Project, in Canada,[1] which makes maps and geospatial information accessible online through the use of scalable vector graphic (SVG) maps, which can be magnified without losing the visual quality, together with audio, haptic and tactile output. While these examples are taken from museums and galleries, the innovations could be transferred to a library setting where, for example, special collections are presented online.

The Swedish Library of talking Books and Braille (TPB)[2] has created a website for children (up to 12 years old), which has taken accessibility into account in some innovative ways to produce a site that is attractive and fun for children and includes a lot of graphical images with the aim of motivating children with dyslexia. As well as this, the designers have 'been anxious to write informative and amusing alternative text to these pictures' (Nilsson, 2006). The entire TPB website provides in-built speech so that visitors do not need to have their own speech synthesizer to be able to listen. The website provides talking books with sound illustrations, different narrators and music. The web pages also include a character called Topsy who has been created to encourage children to read. Topsy is a virtual mole who reads

Braille and talking books and is designed in a way that is also suited to children with partial sight.

Pateman and Newby (2004) report that Nordic libraries have developed websites to enable access for users who are not able to visit the library, and thus to make their services more inclusive. An example is given of Silkeborg library website, which allows users to control many features of their individual library account. A brief exploration of a sample of UK public websites (taken from UK Public Library Websites[3]) reveals further evidence of attempts to widen provision to web services. Manchester City Council Library and Information Service[4] provides information about the accessibility and usability of its website. It includes explanations about the commitment to providing accessible and usable web-based services, how the service strives to achieve this through the use of different design techniques, and how visitors can improve their experience through, for example, changing the font size. Bexley Council Library and Community Information Services website[5] has a help page for visually impaired people, which provides advice on 'things you can do if our pages are hard to read'. This includes information about which web browsers work best and which settings can be adjusted. It also provides step-by-step guidance on setting screen resolutions, display settings and text sizes. Anglesey County Council, which includes information on library and information services,[6] provides an explanation of why it aims to make the website as accessible as possible, citing the WAI and government guidelines. The page then goes on to provide advice on various features of the website, such as the text-only version (using BETSIE), how to adjust the size of the text in various browsers (Internet Explorer and Mozilla Firefox), use of text descriptions for images, how to download PDF documents, Access Keys and how to print out documents and pages. It also provides a link to the webmaster for feedback and reporting problems.

IFLA checklist

Forrest (2005) describes how the Fife Campus library at the School of Nursing and Midwifery, University of Dundee, applied the IFLA checklist 'Access to libraries for persons with disabilities' (Irvall and Nielsen, 2005), which helped the library to build a framework for continued development and improvement. The checklist evaluation revealed evidence of good practice in the library - in particular the provision of web-based resources such as the e-journals and e-books accessed via the library website using magnification and screenreading software installed on the PCs.

The IFLA checklist covers various accessibility areas, such as physical access, media formats, and service and communication, under which the accessibility of the website falls (Irvall and Nielsen, 2005; see also Chapter 7, section on 'Advice and guidelines').

The checklist covers some of the key accessibility issues that need to be addressed, but it should be noted that it does not refer to providing alternative text for graphics and images, an important accessibility consideration for people using screenreading technologies. The guidelines provide a link to the W3C/WAI and to an automated web accessibility checker, but would be of further benefit by providing a brief explanation of why the accessibility points identified are important and how they help to improve access to websites, as this would help increase an understanding of accessibility issues.

Guidelines and advice

Brief explanations to support guidelines and specifications are provided in a set of standards developed by the Japanese government relating to accessibility: 'JIS X 8341: Guidelines for older persons and persons with disabilities - Information and communications equipment, software and services', and more specifically Part 3: (JIS X 8341-3: 2004) 'Web content', which provides brief but helpful explanations of why the web accessibility specifications should be applied to different areas of web design, such as document structure, images, navigation and language (Koga, 2006). The JIS X 8341-3 takes into account international work such as that of the W3C/WAI, but adds some points that are specific to Japan in terms of the text and languages. This demonstrates good practice in developing guidelines and standards relevant to specific national needs.

In Finland, guidelines for accessible web pages were produced in 1997 by the Celia Library. These have been enhanced by the provision of help and training to raise public awareness. Since the production of the guidelines, the Celia Library's web pages have continued to follow the three main design principles: accessibility, usability and Design for All (Zansen, 2006).

The Lancashire County Council website[7] also provides advice on web standards, explaining how the council has been developing web standards and policies to ensure the website (including the library website) is accessible to all and meets government standards. It provides some rules which the council bears in mind when creating web-based content, such as the provision of alterative text for non-textual information; the use of clear and accurate headings and link descriptions; dividing large blocks of text into more manageable sections; and clearly defining the target of each hypertext link.

Raising awareness of accessibility

It is important to ensure that people who are designing or commissioning websites are aware of the issues involved in creating accessible websites. Surveys have shown that awareness of web accessibility and some of the issues does exist. For example, in 2005 the SupportEAM project[8] conducted an online survey on stakeholders' needs for a European eAccessibility certification scheme. The survey revealed that 80% (of the 450 respondents) said that they took accessibility into account when commissioning their websites, but of these only 35% said they checked them for accessibility. 75% of the respondents also stated that they would like to have some kind of methodology and criteria to achieve eAccessibility certification of their websites. Another survey of web designers, developers and web service providers, undertaken to establish the need for the proposed European Internet Accessibility Observatory (Craven and Snaprud, 2005), also showed that the stakeholders surveyed had an understanding of the importance of accessibility issues and of methods available to help and guide them towards creating better websites.

In Japan, research into the uptake of the web accessibility standard undertaken in 2005 (Koga, 2006) revealed that although 74% of local governments in Japan knew about web accessibility, of these only 28% knew the details of the 'JIS X 8341: Guidelines for older persons and persons with disabilities - Information and communications equipment, software and services', and more specifically Part 3: (JIS X 8341-3: 2004) 'Web content'. Worse still, 33.3% were not even aware of the guidelines.

This raises questions as to why accessible design is not spreading more rapidly, and suggests that further research is needed to discover why this is the case and to make recommendations accordingly. Analysis of a web developer questionnaire distributed to partners of the ENABLED project (a three-year EU-funded project which aimed to improve access to the web by blind and visually impaired people), revealed that of the 269 responses, only 36% indicated that they tried to make their websites or applications accessible.[9] The main reason given for not doing this was a lack of knowledge, in particular relating to accessibility features in website development tools. This lack of knowledge could be because only 13% of respondents said they had received any training in accessibility or usability and this could also account for why so many websites are still not as accessible as they could or should be (see also Chapter 4, section on 'Barriers to adoption of web accessibility').

To address the lack of awareness of accessibility issues and relevant guidelines in Japan, an operational model to improve the accessibility of public websites has been developed by the Ministry of Internal Affairs and Communications, which covers the 'lifecycle of government Website management' (Koga, 2006, 11). Some of the measures recommended in the operational model are:

- training programmes and learning materials for government staff
- evaluation measures of web accessibility skills for technical staff
- common infrastructures and resources to ensure web accessibility, such as the templates of web pages
- environment of web accessibility evaluation, such as a 'pool' of monitors consisting of people with disabilities and elderly people
- measures to evaluate web accessibility regularly and efficiently.

(Koga, 2006, 12).

In Europe, recommendations from the UK Cabinet Office report on the accessibility of public sector services in the European Union (covering libraries), conducted during the UK presidency of the EU in 2005, include:

- Recommendation 6: Carry out a feasibility study in 2006 into the development of an appropriate qualification in accessible websites for developers, managers and content providers (perhaps aligned with the European Computer Driving Licence).
- Recommendation 10: Produce a plan for improving awareness throughout the country by reviewing all the examples of engagement identified in this survey as ideas for improving awareness of web accessibility.
- Recommendation 15: Make sure that all content commissioners and authors are fully trained in the importance of accessible content, and in

the means that are made available to them to achieve this.

- Recommendation 19: Train all web designers in both the requirement for, and the techniques to achieve, fully accessible websites.
- Recommendation 20: Develop a competence framework for web designers, which includes web accessibility, and use it for personal development schemes and recruitment campaigns.

(Cabinet Office, 2005, 60-2).

Web accessibility studies

Library website accessibility

A number of studies have been conducted on the accessibility of websites to explore whether the increased promotion of accessibility issues and Design for All have improved the design and development of websites. In 1999 two studies of library websites in the UK (Brophy and Craven, 1999; Ormes and Peacock, 1999) revealed that accessible design was only in the early stages of development, displaying low levels of accessibility in the websites that were assessed. In 2002 Kelly studied the accessibility of UK university home pages using an automated accessibility checker (Kelly, 2002). The study revealed that despite a move towards the design of accessible web pages, many did not fully comply with the recommendations of the Web Accessibility Initiative Web Content Accessibility Guidelines (WCAG).

A 2005 study of UK public library catalogues (Palfery, 2005) found that most libraries were not meeting the requirements of the Disability Discrimination Act 1995. The catalogues were first checked against the WAI standards (WCAG 1.0) and using an automated web accessibility checker; manual testing was undertaken using a text-only browser; structured user testing was performed with a small sample of visually impaired volunteers; and finally, non-web-based catalogues were checked to see whether they were more accessible than the web versions.

Findings showed that the more recent catalogues took into account accessibility features such as contrasting colours and adjustable settings. However, none of the catalogues tested reached the WCAG level AA standards and user testing revealed further problems with language, layout and general information overload. The study placed blame for these failures on the libraries (lack of awareness of accessibility recommendations, use of library-related jargon), councils (lack of standard HTML) and - more significantly - the library suppliers: 'none of them offer a standard system that is fully level-AAA compliant . . .' (Palfery, 2005, 33). Recommendations for improvements included:

- put pressure on your supplier to improve the accessibility of the catalogue - or consider changing supplier
- reduce the number of links on menus and provide menu skipping links
- validate HTML and accessibility using automated tools
- don't sacrifice accessibility for security
- test systems with the help of at least one visually impaired person.

Another study of disabled people's experiences using the internet (Pilling, Barrett and Floyd, 2004) revealed that they would like websites to include the following:

- guides on the home page informing people about the sites' contents
- less cluttered pages
- fewer graphics and less advertising
- links to be clearer and fewer
- print size and colours to be easily changeable
- greater standardization
- search to be more clearly marked and more precise
- better accessibility for voice recognition system users.

(Pilling, Barrett and Floyd, 2004, 34)

People using assistive technologies described the problems they experienced accessing the internet. For example, screen magnification 'looks a bit fuzzy when it's blown up' (ibid., 2004, 30). Problems with screenreaders were described, as well as inability to afford the more up-to-date technologies such as JAWS (ibid., 2004, 32). Lack of support and training in the use of assistive technologies was identified as another barrier to access.

Large-scale web accessibility studies

City University in the UK tested the accessibility of a sample of museum, library and archive websites in England and internationally (City University, 2004). Automated testing revealed that only a small number (3%) of websites met the WCAG accessibility level AA (level AAA being the highest level, and level A the most basic level of accessibility). Also in 2004, a formal investigation of web accessibility was commissioned by the Disability Rights Commission (DRC). The study used a sample of 1000 websites, which were tested first using an automated software tool and then evaluated by 50 users with a variety of impairments (DRC, 2004). The study identified 585 accessibility and usability problems, the most common of which related to the following eight WCAG checkpoints:

- Checkpoint 1.1: Provide a text equivalent for every non-text element.
- Checkpoint 2.2: Ensure foreground and background colour combinations provide sufficient colour contrast etc.
- Checkpoint 6.3: Ensure pages are usable when scripts etc. are turned off, and if this is not possible provide an alternative.
- Checkpoint 7.3: Until user agents allow users to freeze moving content, avoid movement in pages.
- Checkpoint 10.1: Until user agents allow users to turn off spawned windows, do not cause pop ups without informing the user.
- Checkpoint 12.3: Divide large blocks of information into more manageable groups where natural and appropriate.
- Checkpoint 13.1: Clearly identify the target of each link.
- Checkpoint 14.1: Use the clearest and simplest language appropriate for a site's content.

(DRC, 2004)

As part of the UK Presidency of the EU, in 2005 the UK Cabinet Office was commissioned to evaluate the accessibility of government online services across Europe (Cabinet Office, 2005). These findings revealed that only 3% of the 436 online websites assessed achieved the most basic level of WCAG (A) and none achieved level AA.

Web accessibility initiatives and projects

eEurope Action plans

To increase use of the internet in all areas of European society, member states of the EU are required to adhere to the eEurope Action Plan (European Commission, 2002). The Action Plan recommends the adoption of the Web Accessibility Initiative (WAI) guidelines and the development of a European

Design for All curriculum, strengthening assistive technology and Design for All standardization. Recommendations are also made relating to the procurement of accessible public information and communication technologies, along the same lines as the Section 508 legislation in the USA, which requires the procurement of electronic and information technologies that are accessible to people with disabilities.

Since 2002, the European Commission has disseminated a Communication on eAccessibility which aims to move forward the recommendations of the Action Plan and to achieve 'an "Information Society for All", promoting an inclusive digital society that provides opportunities for all and minimizes the risk of exclusion' (European Commission, 2005a). The measures recommended by the Commission include Design for All methods in the design of products and services, including the design and evaluation of websites and drawing on recommendations made by the W3C/WAI. At present e-Accessibility is still required on a voluntary basis, but if sufficient progress has not been made by the planned review of progress, then legislative action may have to be considered.

Web accessibility benchmarking

As part of the European Commission Information Society Technologies (IST) programme of research to support e-inclusion, accessible web design, development and assessment has been the focus of a Web Accessibility Benchmarking (WAB) cluster of three EU-funded projects working to develop a harmonized European methodology for evaluation and benchmarking of websites: the 'Unified Web Accessibility Methodology' or UWEM.[10] The cluster projects are looking at three specific areas:

1. The European Internet Accessibility Observatory (EIAO): To provide an online web accessibility assessment tool which provides indications of the accessibility of public websites over time, via a user interface. The aim of this project is to allow people with web responsibilities to track the accessibility of their website, and to compare them with other websites within their sector (e.g. libraries), region and country.
2. SupportEAM: Investigation of a possible web accessibility quality mark (proposal of a certification mechanism and authority, national helpdesks, training material etc.).
3. BenToWeb: Production of test suites for evaluation tools, and evaluation

modules for checkpoints difficult to automate; research into integration of testing modules in content management systems (CMS) and issues related to dynamic multi-version web pages.

By co-ordinating aspects of the work described above, the three projects will work together to develop an EU-harmonized assessment methodology for web accessibility, based on W3C/WAI and to be synchronized with the move from WCAG1.0 to WCAG2.0.

Web accessibility standards

To further the aim to create an information society for all, the European Commission has issued a mandate to three European standardization organizations - the European Committee for Standardization (CEN), the European Committee for Electrotechnical Standardization (CENELEC) and the European Telecommunications Standards Institute (ETSI) - to establish standards in support of European accessibility requirements for public procurement of ICT products and services. The objectives of the mandate are to harmonize and facilitate the public procurement of accessible ICT products by identifying a set of accessibility requirements. These will be used to provide an electronic toolkit which will enable public procurers to implement the accessibility requirements in a harmonized way. The requirements will take into account issues relating to assistive technologies and Design for All. The mandate will be carried out in two phases:

1. Phase 1: An inventory of European and international accessibility requirements and assessment of suitable testing and conformity schemes.
2. Phase 2: Standardization activities to support work undertaken in Phase 1. Included in this will be an online toolkit providing access to a European Standard of technical specifications for public procurement which corresponds with requirements identified for accessibility; guidelines on accessibility criteria; and guidance and support material for public procurements.

(European Commission, 2005b).

Involving users in accessibility assessments

Assessment methods

Methods for assessing and testing accessibility and usability are well documented (see Chapter 5). For example, see resources such as the W3C Web Accessibility Initiative guidelines and techniques;[11] *PAS 78: Guide to good practice in commissioning accessible websites*;[12] the Web Standards project;[13] Jakob Nielsen's Usability Heuristics (Nielsen, 1994, 155); as well as automated checkers such as WAVE[14] and Cynthia Says[15] (see also Chapter 6). But, again, this has not resulted in a significant increase in the accessibility of web-based information (Nomensa, 2006; Cabinet Office, 2005; City University, 2004).

Importance of user involvement

Accessibility studies have shown that it is important also to involve users in the process as their experience may differ from the automated assessments. The European Internet Accessibility Observatory (EIAO) project has set out to try to identify more generally what users want from an accessible website and the problems they have encountered (Craven and Snaprud, 2005). Having established general requirements and problems experienced through a survey and a series of interviews with end-users, the project compared and identified relevant checkpoints based on the WCAG. The findings influenced the technical development of the project in terms of interface and schema design. Also, by identifying statements provided by the users, a clearer picture was provided of what users actually want to get from an accessible website, rather than making assumptions.

Incorrect assumptions were identified in a study by the Memorial University of Newfoundland (MUN) (McGillis and Toms, 2001), where participants undertook user testing of the library website. The main problem identified was that people did not know where to start, often because the language used on the website was confusing, even if it was well established terminology. No user testing had ever been conducted on the library website and therefore it was concluded that incorrect assumptions had been made about library users' extent of knowledge when visiting the site, which had led to poor design decisions (McGillis and Toms, 2001, 365).

Another example of the benefits of user testing is the evaluation of an online database conducted by Van House (1995). The development team had made initial assumptions as to what user requirements would be, but the assessments revealed a variety of needs that differed between groups of users (library staff, information officers, lawyers etc.), thus indicating that requirements need to be defined more specifically, and that they vary from group to group. A particular emphasis is given to an iterative approach – where assessment and evaluation of digital library design takes place 'before, during and after design, with the emphasis on before and during' (Van House, 1995).

User surveys and user testing

A survey of the experiences of blind and visually impaired people using electronic information services (Lewis, 2004) found that adherence to accessibility guidelines will not ensure that services are usable for blind and visually impaired people. Feedback from real users is essential, alongside automated testing of websites, to ensure that guidelines are valid and relevant. Unfamiliarity with electronic equipment and lack of support and training in its use were also identified as barriers to accessibility.

Involving people with different access requirements (such as disabled people or people using alternative devices such as a mobile phone) will also provide a much richer insight into the accessibility of a web page. Nielsen recommends at least 15 users to discover all the usability design problems; however, he also suggests that excellent results can be gained from using as few as five users (Nielsen, 2000). Other studies (DRC, 2004) suggest the majority of accessibility barriers can be identified by using blind and visually impaired people in user testing and accessibility evaluations.

The Non-visual Access to the Digital Library study (Craven and Brophy, 2003) looked at the user behaviour of visually impaired people when accessing and interacting with web-based information. It provided an insight to the types of problems faced by users. The focus of the project was on the information-seeking behaviour of blind and visually impaired people, but the control group of sighted users also highlighted usability problems, thus reinforcing the importance of involving all types of user in any design and development project. The study showed that although awareness of web accessibility is increasing, all types of user can be faced with navigational problems. Some problems experienced are due to accessibility and usability conflicts, such as inappropriate or unhelpful use of alternative text, or poor use of language. Other problems identified are due to a lack of understanding of the different ways users interact with and navigate around web-based resources (Craven and Brophy, 2003, 115, 118; Craven and Griffiths, 2001, 173–86).

Task-based user testing

A task-based approach to user testing has frequently been used as a method of assessing the accessibility and/or usability of websites. For example, McGillis and Toms (2001) used this approach to assess the usability of an academic library website. This involved faculty staff and students who undertook a series of typical tasks to assess success in the completion of tasks and thus to better understand the usability of the site. Others who have used this approach include Borlund and Ingwersen (1997), who developed a 'simulated work task situation' to help dispel feelings among the users in the study that they were being tested in any way. A study of the information-seeking behaviour of visually impaired people in web-based environments (Craven, 2003), where a set of tasks covered broad subject areas such as searching for a weather forecast, shopping for clothes, and seeking travel information, enabled comparative analysis between the information-seeking behaviour of the sighted and visually impaired participants. Craven and Booth (2006) described the methods and findings of two research projects undertaken to explore user behaviour and usability issues relating to the use of web-based resources by people with disabilities. A practical approach to user testing is described, identifying key issues for consideration:

- objectives of the test
- number and type of participants
- recruiting participants
- pilot testing
- ethical issues
- the testing
- transcription and analysis of data
- presentation of findings.

(See also Chapter 6, section on 'User evaluations with disabled people'.)

Summary

Despite the fact that surveys and audits on the accessibility of websites show the situation is not improving at a significant rate, there are examples of good (or best) practice. This chapter has sought to provide evidence of this within the library and information sector.

Examples of innovative ways to enhance the web experience for everyone can be found, as well as examples of how advice and guidelines have been put into practice. Studies into web accessibility help to increase understanding of the issues and provide recommendations based on their findings. Web accessibility projects and initiatives, such as those funded and undertaken by the European Commission, provide evidence of the importance of accessible web design in widening electronic access for as many people as possible. All the examples provided in this chapter are intended to inform and inspire future activities relating to accessible web design and development.

To conclude, the following suggestions are provided for making the web accessible to everyone, and encompass some of the issues and findings described in this chapter. These suggestions are of particular relevance because they are made from the perspective of a blind librarian (Lewis and Klauber, 2002):

- Staff members, consultants and companies that develop library websites should be educated about accessibility standards and how to implement them.
- Team work should be encouraged between library staff involved in developing and maintaining library websites, selecting and purchasing software, and training.
- End-users should be involved in the processes mentioned above.
- Library staff need to understand how people use assistive technologies.
- Library staff should purchase software etc. only from vendors who guarantee their product's accessibility.

References

Borlund, P. and Ingwersen, P. (1997) The Development of a Method for the Evaluation of Interface Information Retrieval Systems, *Journal of Documentation*, **53** (3), 225–46.

Brophy, P. (2006) *Measuring Library Performance: principles and techniques*, London, Facet Publishing.

Brophy, P. and Craven, J. (1999) *The Integrated Accessible Library: a model of service development for the 21st Century*, British Library Research and Innovation Report 168, Manchester, Centre for Research in Library and Information Management (CERLIM).

Cabinet Office (2005) e-Accessibility of Public Sector Services in the European Union, www.rnib.org.uk/xpedio/groups/public/documents/publicwebsite/public_euacc.pdf.

City University (2004) *Accessibility of Museum, Library and Archive Websites: the MLA audit*, London, Centre for Human Computer Interaction Design.

Craven, J. (2003) Access to Electronic Resources by Visually Impaired People, *Information Research*, **8** (4), http://informationr.net/ir/8-4/paper156.html.

Craven, J. and Booth, H. (2006) Putting Awareness into Practice: practical steps for conducting usability tests, *Library Review*, **55** (3), 179–94.

Craven, J. and Brophy, P. (2003) *Non-visual Access to the Digital Library: the use of digital library interfaces by blind and visually impaired people*, Library and Information Commission Report 145, Manchester, Centre for Research in Library and Information Management (CERLIM).

Craven, J. and Griffiths, J. (2001) 30,000 Different Users, 30,000 Different Needs? The design and delivery of distributed resources to your user community. In Brophy, P., Fisher, S. and Clarke, Z. (eds), *Libraries Without Walls: the delivery of library services to distant users: proceedings of the 4th Libraries Without Walls Conference, 14–18 September 2001*, London, Facet Publishing, 173–86.

Craven, J. and Snaprud, M. (2005) Involving Users in the Development of a Web Accessibility Tool, *Ariadne*, **44**, 30 July, www.ariadne.ac.uk/issue44/craven/intro.html.

Disability Rights Commission (DRC) (2004) *The Web: access and inclusion for disabled people*, London, The Stationery Office.

ENABLED Web Developer Survey, www.enabledweb.org/public_results/survey_results/analysis.html.

European Commission (2002) *eEurope 2002: accessibility of public websites and their content*, COM (2001) 529.

European Commission (2005a) *Communication from the Commission to the Council, the European Parliament, the Economic and Social Committee, and the Committee of Regions: eAccessibility*, COM (2005) 42.5.

European Commission (2005b) *Standardisation Mandate to CEN, CENELEC and ETSI in Support of European Accessibility Requirements for Public Procurement of Products and Services in the ICT Domain*, M 376-EN, Brussels, 7 December 2005.

Forrest, M. E. S. (2005) Towards an Accessible Academic Library: using the IFLA checklist, IFLANET, 10 June, www.ifla.org/V/iflaj/IFLA-Journal-1-2006.pdf.

Irvall, B. and Nielsen, G. S. (2005) Access to Libraries for Persons with Disabilities - checklist, IFLA Professional Reports 89, International Federation of Library Associations and Institutions.

Kelly, B. (2002) WebWatch: an accessibility analysis of UK university entry points, *Ariadne*, **33**, www.ariadne.ac.uk/issue33/web-watch/.

Koga, T. (2006) Policy Issues Regarding Electronic Government and Web Accessibility in Japan. In WILIC *72nd General Conference and Council, 20-24 August 2006, Seoul, Korea*, www.ifla.org/IV/ifla72/index.htm.

Lewis, A. (2004) A User Survey of the Experiences of Blind and Visually Impaired People Using Electronic Information Services with Regard to the Practical Implementation of these Services in Public Libraries, MSc dissertation, Robert Gordon University, Aberdeen Business School, Department of Information Management.

Lewis, V. and Klauber, J. (2002) [Image] [Image] [Image] [Link] [Link] [Link]: inaccessible web design from the perspective of a blind librarian, *Library Hi Tech*, **20** (2), 137-40.

McGillis, L. and Toms, E. G. (2001) Usability of the Academic Library Web Site: implications for design, *College and Research Libraries*, July, 355-67.

Nielsen, J. (1994) *Usability Engineering*, Morgan Kaufman.

Nielsen, J. (2000) *Designing Web Usability*, Indianapolis, New Riders Publishing.

Nilsson, J. (2006) The Children's TPB - an Open Window for Children with Print Impairments. In WILIC, *72nd General Conference and Council, 20-24 August 2006, Seoul, Korea*, www.ifla.org/IV/ifla72/index.htm.

Nomensa (2006) *United Nations Global Audit of Web Accessibility*, www.nomensa.com/resources/research/united-nations-global-audit-of-accessibility.html.

Ormes, S. and Peacock, I. (1999) Virtually Inaccessible to All? *Library Technology*, **4** (1), 17-18.

Palfery, R. (2005) Access Denied: catalogue accessibility for VIPs, *Update*, **4** (3), 32-3.

Pateman, J. and Newby, C. (2004) The Essence of Inclusion: Cuba and the Nordic states, *Update*, **3** (11), 30-3.

Pilling, D., Barrett, P. and Floyd, M. (2004) *Disabled People and the Internet: experiences, barriers and opportunities*, Joseph Rowntree Foundation.

Van House, N. (1995) User Needs Assessment and Evaluation for the UC Berkeley Electronic Environmental Library Project: a preliminary report. In *Digital Libraries '95: the Second International Conference on the Theory and*

Practice of Digital Libraries, June 11–13, 1995, Austin, TX, http://csdl.tamu.edu/DL95/papers/vanhouse/vanhouse.html.

Walsh, J. (2006) Improving Web Accessibility for the Visually Impaired, *Library Hi Tech News*, **8**, 29–31.

Wikipedia, http://en.wikipedia.org/wiki/Best_practice (accessed 2007).

Zansen, M. von (2006) Accessibility as a Prerequisite for Library Web Services. In WILIC, *72nd General Conference and Council, 20–24 August 2006, Seoul, Korea*, www.ifla.org/IV/ifla72/index.htm.

URLs

1 http://tactile.nrcan.gc.ca/page.cgi?url=projet_project/index_e.html
2 www.tpb.se/english
3 http://dspace.dial.pipex.com/town/square/ac940/weblibs.html
4 www.manchester.gov.uk/libraries
5 www.bexley.gov.uk/service/library.html
6 www.ynysmon.gov.uk/doc.asp?cat=1213&Language=1
7 www.lancashire.gov.uk/libraries/index.asp
8 www.support-eam.org
9 www.enabledweb.org/download/HFT06_Paper.pdf
10 www.wabcluster.org
11 www.w3.org/WAI/guid-tech.html
12 www.equalityhumanrights.com/en/publicationsandresources/Disability/Pages/Websiteaccessibilityguidance.aspx
13 www.webstandards.org
14 www.wave.webaim.org/index.jsp
15 www.icdri.org/test_your_site_now.htm

Chapter 10

Web accessibility in the future

BRIAN KELLY

Introduction

This final chapter will take a critical look at some of the developments in web accessibility guidelines and assessment, and will provide some suggestions as to how these could be improved, in particular through a more holistic approach to web accessibility. It will then move on to consider accessibility issues surrounding the new emerging technologies and how these might relate to library and information services.

We have seen how the guidelines developed by the World Wide Web Consortium (W3C) Web Accessibility Initiative (WAI) have been widely accepted as an international standard for helping to ensure that web resources can be made widely accessible. But how successful has this approach proved in practice? And will the WAI guidelines continue to be relevant in a rapidly changing technical environment, in particular in a Web 2.0 environment with increasing use of technologies such as blogs and wikis, communication tools such as instant messaging and internet telephony applications such as Skype?

A critique of the WAI approach

WAI has been tremendously successful in raising awareness of the need for access to web resources for people with disabilities and in encouraging governments to enshrine such commitments in legislation, with WAI's Web Content Accessibility Guidelines (WCAG) having been widely adopted as best practice for use by web content providers (see Chapter 5, section on 'The Web Accessibility Initiative Guidelines').

However, even among individuals and groups who may be committed to web accessibility principles, there are growing criticisms regarding the approaches taken by WAI. Researchers and accessibility practitioners in the UK (including the author of this chapter) have been exploring these limitations, which include inconsistencies and ambiguities in the guidelines, the failure of the guidelines to reflect technological developments, and the diverse ways in which the web is now being used.

As described in a paper by Kelly et al. (2005), the approach developed by WAI is a simple model based on three components (illustrated in Figure 10.1): guidelines for web content (WCAG), guidelines for authoring tools (ATAG) and guidelines for user agents such as web browsers (UAAG). The assumption is that if authors follow the web content authoring guidelines using authoring tools that are based on ATAG and users make use of browsers that are based on UAAG then the resources will be universally accessible.

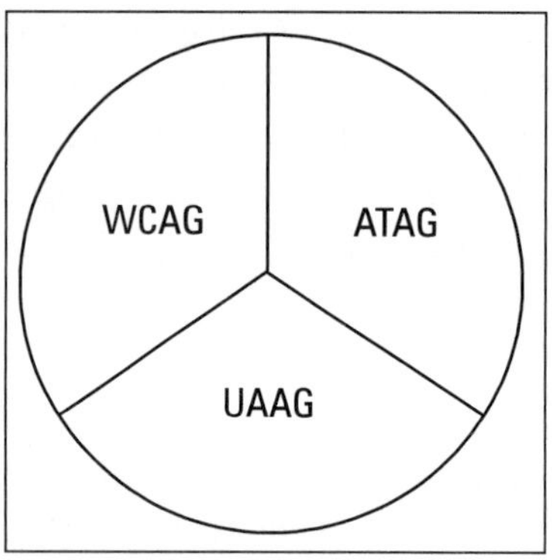

Figure 10.1 The WAI model

In reality this approach is far too simplistic. Browsers that provide full support for various accessibility features (including Cascading Style Sheets) are not widely available and, in any case, institutions face various constraints in managing the web browser environment on an enterprise scale. There is also the issue of the many users (particularly in a home environment) who may be reluctant to install a new browser and may be happy to use the default browser.

There are similar problems with HTML authoring tools and content management systems that may be needed to enable accessible content to be created. Many large-scale content management systems, for example, fail to address basic requirements such as generating compliant HTML and CSS resources.

In addition to the constraints of the market place (vendors who may find it difficult to, or are unwilling to, develop products that comply with WAI's ATAG and UAAG guidelines) and the difficulties institutions may have in deploying software (when and if such software exists) that provides better support for such guidelines, we must not forget that end-users of browsers and authoring tools may also be reluctant to migrate to new applications, preferring instead the applications they are familiar with (see also Chapter 4, section on 'Barriers to adoption of web accessibility').

Limitations of the WAI WCAG

Authors of web resources are thus restricted in what they can do to enhance the accessibility of their web services to ensuring that their resources comply with WCAG. This might not be a problem if there were general agreement that these guidelines worked. However, there are problems with the guidelines, including difficulties in understanding them ('what does it mean?') and in interpreting them ('must I do this in all circumstances?') and logical flaws.

A number of limitations with WCAG 1.0 are summarized below.

Theoretical nature

Many HTML authors, including those who are well disposed to enhancing the accessibility of their resources, feel that the guidelines are too theoretical and are based on a W3C perspective of how the web should work rather than real-world experiences of how the web is actually being used. For example, WCAG 1.0 supporting documentation makes no mention of widely used web formats such as PDF and Flash, concentrating instead on W3C technologies (such as such as RDF, PNG and SVG), which are far from ubiquitous and for which little practical experience may be available within organizations seeking to use the guidelines.

Dependencies on other WAI guidelines

As mentioned above, the WAI model of complementary accessibility guidelines presents accessibility as a tripartite responsibility of users, browser and assistive technology developers, and web content providers. In practice this model is inappropriate for web authors, since developments to web browsers and HTML authoring tools are outside of their control.

Ambiguity

The guidelines themselves are ambiguous. Phrases such as 'until user agents' and 'if appropriate' are used, which can be difficult to define. In an attempt to clarify the diversity of interpretations of WCAG, in 2003 a questionnaire was distributed at an annual UK web management workshop aimed at university web managers.[1] The responses, from an audience with much knowledge of web accessibility issues, showed a diverse set of answers to statements such as 'Testing of accessibility can be fully achieved through the use of automated accessibility checking tools' and 'Fully accessible websites should contain no pictures or multimedia features'.

Complexity

Not only are the WCAG ambiguous, but they are also complex. This has led to many documents being written that seek to explain and interpret the guidelines. However, this then leads to further confusion as such explanatory documents may perpetuate the confusion.

Closed nature

The guidelines require use of W3C formats. Thus they implicitly fail to recognize the increasing emphasis placed on accessibility by vendors of proprietary file formats such as Flash and PDF. The guidelines do not allow web developers to embrace a diversity of solutions in order to provide effective web services to meet a diverse set of requirements, but may be perceived as imposing a W3C-approved solution. The guidelines also fail to acknowledge the accessibility features that may be provided within an operating system environment (which can also help to provide an accessible environment for a range of desktop applications and not just a web browser).

Logical flaws

The wording of the WCAG can lead to a number of logical absurdities. For example, a strict interpretation of the Priority 2 guidelines, which state: 'use the latest versions [of W3C technologies] when supported', would mean that a WCAG Level AA-conformant HTML 4 website would be degraded to WCAG Level A conformance overnight when XHTML 1.0 was officially released! There are similar flaws when one considers use of GIF (a widely used but proprietary graphical format) and PNG (an open and rich, but comparatively rarely used, W3C graphical format). Use of a closed graphical format such as GIF would appear to break the WCAG Priority 2 guideline, which requires web developers to 'Use W3C technologies when they are available and appropriate for a task'. But is there any evidence that use of GIF rather than PNG is a significant accessibility barrier?

Required level of understanding of accessibility issues

It needs to be remembered that the majority of individuals working to make websites accessible, both developers and managers, are not experts in accessibility or in access technologies and never will be. Accessibility is one aspect of developing a website that they are seeking to understand.

Surveys of compliance with WAI WCAG

Various surveys of compliance of web resources with WCAG have shown that compliance levels are poor. The most comprehensive survey was probably the large-scale survey commissioned by the Disability Rights Commission, which reported that 81% of the 1000 websites audited failed to conform with the minimum requirements (level A) of the WCAG (DRC, 2004). The MLA (Museums, Libraries and Archives Council) commissioned another large-scale survey of websites in the cultural heritage sector (Petrie, King and Hamilton, 2005; Weisen et al., 2005). This survey produced more positive findings, but it still found that fewer than half of the websites audited conformed with level A of the WCAG.

Other surveys have been more limited in scope, often using automated accessibility checking tools. Such approaches can only report on possible compliance, since manual checking is needed in order for people to confirm that a resource is accessible. However, surveys that use automated checking tools can be useful because they can provide information on potential compliance with guidelines. Such tools can, for example, report on whether an image has an ALT attribute (which could be used by a screenreader) but cannot state whether the contents of an ALT attribute are useful or not.

A summary of a number of accessibility surveys is given in Table 10.1. These are based on surveys of UK university home pages in 2002 and 2004 (Kelly, 2002, 2004) and of 100 leading international universities (Kane, Shulman and Ladner, 2007).

We might feel that these surveys, which demonstrate the low levels of compliance, show either a lack of knowledge of the guidelines and ways of implementing them or a lack of willingness to implement the guidelines, despite legal requirements in many countries to provide accessible websites. However, an alternative interpretation would be that the low levels of compliance are actually due to the flaws in the guidelines, which have been described above. If this supposition is the case, then we need to ask ourselves how we should go about providing accessible web services.

Table 10.1 Summary of WCAG compliance in various sectors

Sector	WCAG A compliance	WCAG AA compliance	Reference
1000 websites	19%		DRC, 2004
300 museum, library and archive websites	41.6%	3.4%	Petrie, King and Hamilton, 2005 Weisen et al., 2005
UK university home pages	42.9%	2.5%	Kelly, 2002
UK university home pages	57.8%	5.5%	Kelly, 2004
100 leading universities		2%	Kane, Shulman and Ladner, 2007

Building on the WAI approach

In light of the limitations of the WAI approach to web accessibility described above, and the evidence indicating the willingness of public sector organizations to follow best practice in order to widen access to their resources, we need to ask ourselves what should be done. Should we discard the guidelines provided by WAI? Or should we ignore these criticisms, as the guidelines have widespread acceptance and, in many cases, can help to enhance the accessibility of web resources, while turning a blind eye to their limitations?

The approach taken by a group of accessibility researchers and practitioners in the UK has been to build on the political successes of WAI and to support use of WAI guidelines when they can clearly provide accessibility benefits, but to encourage a wider view of the meaning of accessibility and of ways of enhancing accessibility.

Holistic framework for e-learning accessibility

An area in which conflicts with the WAI approach have emerged is that of e-learning, and from this a holistic framework for e-learning accessibility has been developed that could be transferred to the design and development of other e-resources. Developers of e-learning resources needed to consider what approaches should be taken for simple resources that make use of HTML and images, and then to consider making more complex, richly interactive resources accessible, such as a 3D visualization of a molecule.

With a simple resource the obvious answer would be to apply WCAG, providing ALT text for images, for example. However, a possible danger with this approach is that such accessibility information may give away the answer, and therefore subvert the learning process. A question on what feature(s) a diverse series of pictures have in common could be too easy to answer if ALT text (which is accessible to all users) were to emphasize particular features.

The more complex 3D visualization might pose a different set of challenges, not only in the accessibility of the images for visually impaired students, but also in manipulating the user interface for students with physical disabilities. A response to this scenario could be that, because the learning resource cannot be made accessible, it should not be deployed at all. It is self-evident that this would be a foolish decision to make.

A solution to these difficulties has been the development of a holistic framework for e-learning accessibility by Kelly, Phipps and Swift (2004). This approach places emphasis on the learner's needs and recognizes that resource issues, usability and local factors such as the technical infrastructure need to be considered alongside accessibility issues (Figure 10.2).

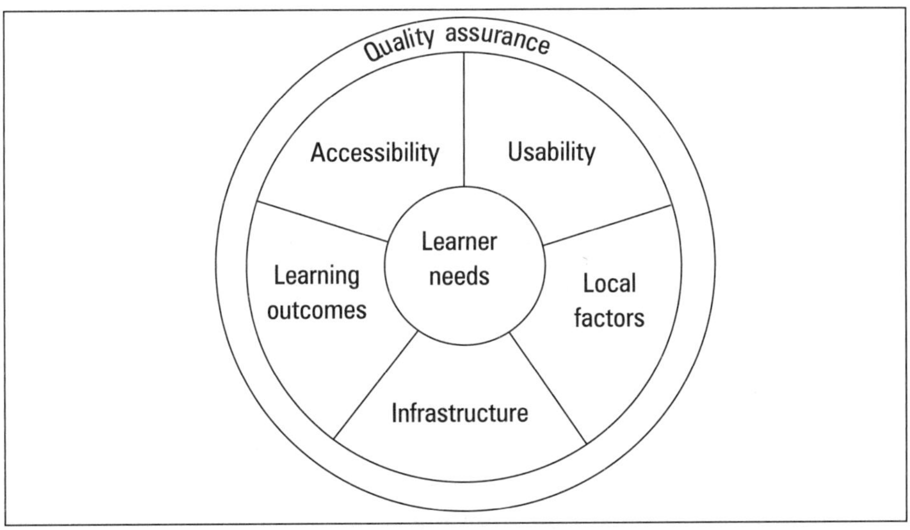

Figure 10.2 Holistic framework for e-learning accessibility

Focusing on the learner's needs rather than on the digital resources allows us to address the accessibility of the learning experiences, rather than the accessibility of the e-learning resources. From this perspective the accessibility of a 3D visualization, such as a molecule, could be addressed by a physical alternative - perhaps, in the case of a course at a school level, use of ping-pong balls and pipe cleaners! Similarly, use of images to generate thinking and, in a group context, discussion and debate, can be addressed by focusing on corresponding group activities.

The term 'blended accessibility' has been coined to describe this approach, which reflects the growing emphasis in the educational sector on 'blended learning' rather than just 'e-learning'.

Extensions to other areas

The application of this holistic approach to e-learning accessibility can be applied in other contexts. How, for example, might you make a surrealist painting by Salvador Dali accessible, a gestalt-style image, such as the duck/rabbit shown in Figure 10.3 or, moving from a visual to a cultural context, a cultural-specific phrase such as 'Super Caley go ballistic Celtic are atrocious' - a pun on the song sung in *Mary Poppins*, which appeared as a headline in the UK newspaper the *Sun*, following football team Caledonian Thistle's unexpected Scottish Cup victory against Glasgow Celtic? This was voted pun of the year in 2000, but is likely to be meaningless for those who are unfamiliar with the film *Mary Poppins*.

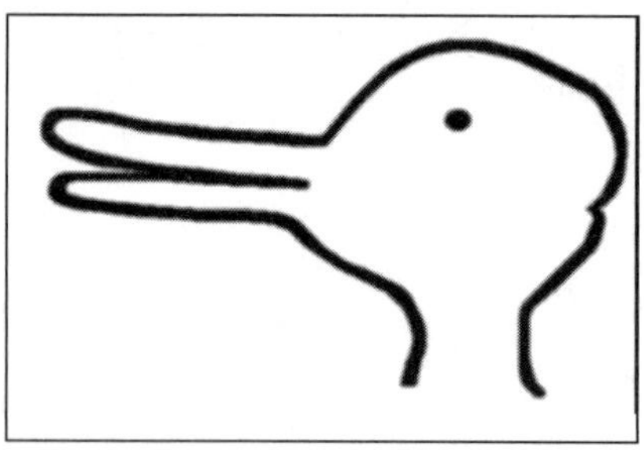

Figure 10.3 What do you see?

With these examples we can see that the notion of 'universal accessibility' is limited. The term may have relevance within the context of strictly informational resources, but even in this area, as we can see from the football headline example, it can be expected that information provided in an amusing or witty form may not be universally accessible.

If the WAI approach breaks in such scenarios, is there a more general framework that can encompass both areas in which application of WAI guidelines can enhance accessibility and areas in which it may be inapplicable or counter-productive?

A metaphor that has been developed by Sloan et al. (2006) to help articulate a more flexible approach is the Tangram Model. Based on the tangram puzzle, which we may remember from our childhood (a cardboard square that is split into seven pieces, which are then used to produce attractive shapes), as shown in Figure 10.4.

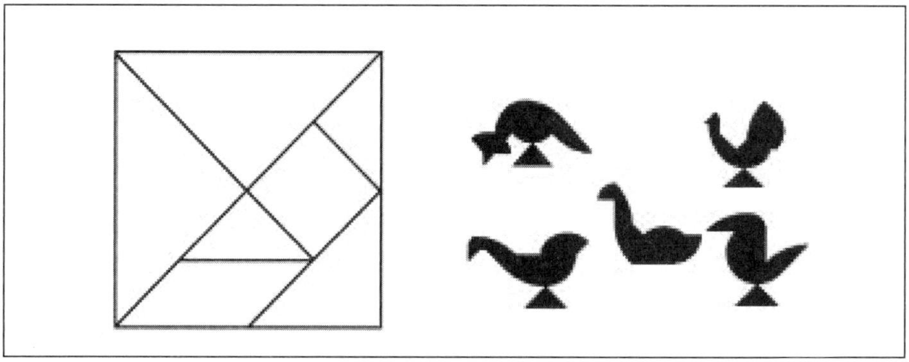

Figure 10.4 Tangram metaphor for accessibility

In this metaphor, the individual pieces can be used to represent various guidelines or best practices such as WCAG, usability and interoperability guidelines, organizational guidelines, guidelines for writing style, etc. The aim is to use the pieces in order to produce a solution that is 'pleasing' to the target audience.

If, say, you wished to produce a poster aimed at teenagers in a deprived inner-city environment, the poster might use language likely to be understood by the target group but which would not necessarily be comprehensible to a wider section of the public. A similar approach would be appropriate for an online marketing campaign, even if the resource was not 'universally accessible'.

This metaphor aims to ensure that a user-focused approach to the application of accessibility guidelines is adopted, rather than the guidelines being used as a formal checklist that must be applied in all cases.

A look to the future

We have described a user-focused approach to web accessibility that treats accessibility guidelines as guidelines, to be used where possible as long as this can be done reasonably. But will this approach be feasible in the future, as technologies develop further, or should we expect the guidelines to be further refined in order to provide an approach to accessibility that is universally consistent?

We should first try to get a feel for how technological developments will change the environment in which we live. If developments continue as expected we can expect to see:

- Pervasive networking: Ubiquitous WiFi provided either for free or at low cost. In addition, further developments to mobile phone technologies which may complement WiFi.
- Multitude of networked devices: Network capabilities will be provided in a whole host of mobile devices (mobile phones, PDAs, music players, digital cameras, etc.) and home equipment (games machines, digital TV, etc.).
- Growth in social networks: Increasing use of social networking environments such as MySpace, Facebook, etc.
- Further Web 2.0 developments: Increasing integration of data ('mashups') together with enhanced usability (through technologies such as AJAX), which will help to transform the web from an informational resource to an application environment.

Rather than a bottom-up approach of examining each of the individual components and exploring how accessibility guidelines could apply to their use, an alternative approach would be to explore the accessibility benefits that such enhancements could provide.

As an example, consider how a popular internet telephony application such as Skype can be used to enhance accessibility. The author has used Skype on a number of occasions to enable remote participants to listen in and contribute to meetings. On one occasion a participant in a meeting on accessibility had problems travelling from Southampton to York due to train delays. It was possible to use Skype to provide what might be called 'just-in-time accessibility'. This richer environment provided not only an audio channel, but also an online chat channel.

Accessibility benefits can also be provided by using social networking environments. Collaborative technologies are being developed that enable communities to annotate images using a variety of keywords. This approach avoids the bottleneck that can occur when the creator of a resource is required to provide metadata, as well as allowing alternative descriptions to be provided.

The key is to first decide what it is you are seeking to achieve with any new service, and then take a broad approach to determine how to maximize the accessibility of those objectives. This is in contrast to interpreting the WAI guidelines as defining what can't be done, which can lead to useful services not being developed. This open approach to accessibility would thus be capable of embracing new technological developments.

Examples of the holistic approach

We will now explore a number of examples of how an open, holistic approach to accessibility may be used.

Institutional repositories services

There is growing interest within educational institutions in the provision of repository services that can provide management and access capabilities for valuable institutional resources such as peer-reviewed papers, theses, project reports, multimedia resources, etc. An institutional e-print repository service, for example, can be used to provide a managed environment for papers that have been submitted to peer-reviewed publications, ensuring that the resource does not disappear if the author leaves the institution. In addition, metadata can be provided for resources stored in a repository service, allowing those resources to be retrieved without relying on the limitations of a general search engine such as Google.

A potential barrier to the deployment of successful e-print repository services is the reluctance of authors of papers to spend time processing their documents for submission to a repository service. This work could include conversion of documents into appropriate file formats and providing metadata to enable them to be readily accessed. A way of minimizing such barriers, in order to maximize the numbers of articles available in an institutional repository, would be to accept submissions in their native file formats (often MS Word or LaTeX) or as Adobe PDF documents. However, this would be likely to result in a repository service that did not comply with accessibility guidelines which expected resources to be available in an open format (such as HTML) and a description of images to be provided for use by assistive technologies.

Does this mean that, unless an alternative approach is taken that mandates that papers submitted to an e-prints repository are converted to HTML and appropriate accessibility metadata provided, institutional repositories should not be deployed - even if this means that the benefits sought by the research community in providing open access to research publications will fail to be realized?

Rather than such a simple binary choice, we should rather explore how the holistic approach can be applied to the scenario. Using this model, based on the principles of 'widening participation' and 'inclusion' within the legal requirements of 'reasonable measures', the following approaches might be applicable:

- User engagement: Talk to representatives of your target user community and discuss with them the aims of your institutional repository and some of the difficulties you may face in deploying a service. Ask them for their views on the difficulties you may face in addressing some of the accessibility issues and on the compromises you may feel are necessary.
- Policies and procedures: Ensure that your institution has documented policies related to the accessibility of the repository service and suitable quality assurance procedures that will ensure the policies are being implemented.
- Education: Ensure that you have training and staff development procedures in place so that the stakeholders are aware of the needs of users with disabilities and the ways in which those needs can be addressed.
- Training: Ensure that suitable training is provided in the use of tools that can enhance the accessibility of resources that may be deposited in institutional repositories and also in the various workflow processes involved in depositing resources.
- Engaging with third-party stakeholders: Ensure that your institution engages with the full range of stakeholders. Within the institution this may include academic departments and researchers, training and development services, and service departments such as IT and the library. It may also include engagement with publishers to make sure, for example, that templates for journal articles are designed to maximize accessibility of papers that use the template.

(See also Chapter 7, 'Issues for Library and Information Services.)

Entertainment

As well as providing educational, cultural and informative services, the web can be used for entertainment and amusement. In a public library, for example, the web may be used by young children. But what are the accessibility challenges that may need to be addressed in this context?

Let us explore the issues using the example of a Flash game that had been developed within a public library and that was described at a Public Library Web Workshop in 2004. The developer described how easy it was to create the game and how popular it was with young children. However, in response to a question about the accessibility of the game, the developer was clearly uneasy about having used Flash, and confessed that it should probably be removed because it did not comply with WCAG 1.0. It does seem unfortunate that a facility that was popular with its target user community should have to be removed from service. So is there an approach that resolves this dilemma?

As with all web development work, the answer lies in looking at the needs of the user. In this example, the game was developed in order to provide something for children to do while their parents were browsing books in the library. So rather than spending time and effort in developing a, possibly expensive, accessible game, it would be reasonable to provide an alternative distraction, such as building blocks or even a bouncy castle. From this perspective we can regard the potential disabled user (who would not be able to use the Flash game) as a user with alternative preferences. This approach avoids the potentially unnecessary expense in developing an accessible web-based game that may never be used.

The need for policies and sharing

Accessibility policies

Reliance on a set of testable rules and checklists may be popular because it avoids the need for discussion and debate on best practice. The proposed holistic approach is intended to be more flexible and user focused. However, adopting this approach will require organizations to provide appropriate documented policies that describe how accessibility issues will be addressed. Within the UK such policies will need to be formulated within the context of disability legislation that requires organizations to take reasonable measures to ensure that people with disabilities are not unfairly discriminated against.

What is 'reasonable' in this context? And what approaches should be taken to the development of such policies? A good starting point is the WCAG. However, in order to provide the flexibility needed to avoid being constrained by the limitations of the guidelines and the variety of solutions that can be used, the policy should provide flexibility in how the WCAG will be used. 'We will seek to comply with WCAG 1.0, may be a useful starting point for an accessibility policy. You may then wish to describe when you may wish to deviate from advice given in the WCAG. For example, you could state: 'In cases in which strict compliance with WCAG 1.0 is not possible, would be inordinately expensive to deploy or would be in conflict with other aspects of our users' needs, we reserve the right not to comply with such guidelines.' (See also Chapter 4, section on 'Lack of organizational support', and Chapter 9, section on 'Accessibility policies'.)

Sharing

A possible danger with this approach is that the flexibility that the holistic approach to accessibility aimed to provide could be used as an opportunity to continue use of existing practices or to develop inaccessible services. The key to addressing this is the legal requirement to take 'reasonable' measures to provide accessible services. The need to have a definition of 'reasonableness' will be understood by those familiar with the UK legal framework, even if the certainties of clear definitions are preferred by those responsible for making policy decisions. Many web developers and users, for example, would argue strongly that it would not be reasonable to develop a service that could run only on Microsoft's Internet Explorer browser. In more complex areas (such as the need to provide transcripts for podcasts, developing functional interactive maps without technologies such as JavaScript, etc.) an understanding of what may be regarded as reasonable is only likely to emerge through discussion and debate - until a test case establishes a precedent in law.

The library sector would therefore benefit from sharing the approaches that are being taken to the development of policies (as would the actual policies), ways of engaging with the user community and the wider set of stakeholders, and examples of successes and, perhaps even more importantly, failures.

Revisiting WAI guidelines

The role of WCAG 2.0

This chapter aims to provide a generic framework for applying best practices that can help to maximize the accessibility of web resources. The valuable work carried out by WAI has been described. The chapter suggests that the

WCAG 1.0 guidelines should be followed when they can clearly help to enhance web accessibility, but that the guidelines themselves are dated and, in addition, may not be applicable in all cases.

The limitations of WCAG 1.0 are now widely accepted and WAI has been developing an updated version, known as WCAG 2.0 (W3C, 2007). WCAG 2.0 introduces four key principles, known by the acronym POUR:

- *Perceivable*: information and user interface components must be perceivable by users.
- *Operable*: user interface components must be operable by users.
- *Understandable*: information and operation of user interface must be understandable by users.
- *Robust*: content must be robust enough that it can be interpreted reliably by a wide variety of user agents, including assistive technologies.

Each principle contains a list of guidelines that address these principles, as summarized below:

Perceivable

- Provide text alternatives for any non-text content so that it can be changed into other forms people need such as large print, Braille, speech, symbols or simpler language.
- Provide synchronized alternatives for multimedia.
- Create content that can be presented in different ways (for example spoken aloud, simpler layout, etc.) without losing information or structure.
- Make it easier for people with disabilities to see and hear content, including separating foreground from background.

Operable

- Make all functionality available from a keyboard.
- Provide users with disabilities enough time to read and use content.
- Do not create content that is known to cause seizures.
- Provide ways to help users with disabilities navigate, find content and determine where they are.

Understandable

- Make text content readable and understandable.
- Make web pages appear and operate in predictable ways.
- Help users avoid and correct mistakes that do occur.

Robust

- Maximize compatibility with current and future user agents, including assistive technologies.

Although a number of additional documents support the WCAG 2.0 guidelines (including advice on how these principles may be implemented using specific technologies), WAI is to be commended for ensuring that the guidelines are more easily understood and provide more flexibility.

Organizations will still, however, need to ensure that the WCAG principles are applied within a particular context of use. If you wish to provide services such as entertainment, quizzes, etc. or educational and cultural resources on, say, surrealist art, you may decide that the principle of 'understanding' may not be applicable.

Summary

This chapter has reviewed some of the limitations of the WAI approach to addressing web accessibility and argued that, in part, the poor levels of compliance with WCAG may be due to flaws in the guidelines themselves. A description has been provided of an alternative, holistic approach to web accessibility that prioritizes the accessibility of the purpose of a web service, rather than the web resources themselves, and describes how organizations can provide blended services that can complement web services.

The importance of taking a practical approach to web accessibility has been emphasized, and a number of examples of such an approach given. Rather than using a checklist approach, this approach encourages engagement with the range of stakeholders who need to be involved in the provision of accessible and sustainable services.

References

DRC (Disability Rights Commission) (2004) *The Web: access and inclusion for disabled people. A formal investigation conducted by the Disability Rights Commission*, www.equalityhumanrights.com/en/publicationsandresources/Disability/Pages/Websiteaccessibilityguidance.aspx.

Kane, S. S., Shulman, K. J. and Ladner, R. (2007) A Web Accessibility Report Card for Top International University Web Sites, *W4A 2007 Communications Paper, May 07–08 2007, Banff, Canada*, www.w4a.info/2007/prog/16-kane.pdf.

Kelly, B. (2002) An Accessibility Analysis of UK University Entry Points, *Ariadne*, **33**, (September), www.ariadne.ac.uk/issue33/web-watch/.

Kelly, B. (2004) *Accessibility Survey of UK University Entry Points*, June, www.ukoln.ac.uk/web-focus/events/workshops/webmaster-2004/talks/phipps-kelly/survey/.

Kelly, B., Phipps, L. and Swift, E. (2004) Developing a Holistic Approach for E-Learning Accessibility, *Canadian Journal of Learning and Technology*, **30** (3), Autumn 2004, www.ukoln.ac.uk/web-focus/papers/cjtl-2004/.

Kelly, B., Sloan, D., Phipps, L., Petrie, H. and Hamilton, F. (2005) Forcing Standardization or Accommodating Diversity? A framework for applying the WCAG in the real world, *Proceedings of the 2005 International Cross-Disciplinary Workshop on Web Accessibility (W4A)*, www.ukoln.ac.uk/web-focus/papers/w4a-2005.

Petrie, H., King, N. and Hamilton, F. (2005) *Accessibility of Museum, Library and Archive Websites: the MLA audit*, www.mla.gov.uk/website/policy/Diversity/Web_Accessibility.

Sloan, D., Kelly, B., Heath, A., Petrie, H., Hamilton, F. and Phipps, L. (2006) Contextual Web Accessibility - maximizing the benefit of accessibility guidelines, *WWW 2006 Edinburgh, Scotland 22–26 May 2006. Conference Proceedings, Special Interest Tracks, Posters and Workshops* (CD ROM), www.ukoln.ac.uk/web-focus/papers/w4a-2006/.

Weisen, M., Petrie, H., King, N. and Hamilton, F. (2005) Assibility Revealed: the Museums, Libraries and Archives Council audit, *Ariadne*, **44** (July), www.ariadne.ac.uk/issue44/petrie-weisen/.

W3C (2007) *Web Content Accessibility Guidelines 2.0, W3C Working Draft 17 May 2007*, www.w3.org/TR/WCAG20/.

URLs

1 www.ukoln.ac.uk/web-focus/events/workshops/webmaster-2003/accessibility-questionnaire/

Index